Scaling Your Social Venture

Social Entrepreneurship

Series Editors:

Paul N. Bloom, Adjunct Professor of Social Entrepreneurship and Marketing, Duke University's Fuqua School of Business, Faculty Director of CASE

Matt Nash, Managing Director of CASE

Social entrepreneurship is a growing field of practice and scholarship. Spurred by the financial support and encouragement of organizations like the Skoll Foundation, Ashoka, the Schwab Foundation, Echoing Green, and the Acumen Fund, many individuals and organizations have labeled themselves as "social entrepreneurs" and are drawing upon the best thinking in both the business and philanthropic worlds to develop innovative approaches to addressing critical social needs in health, poverty, the environment, and other domains. With this growth in the number of practitioners has come a concomitant growth in the number of students, consultants, teachers, and researchers who want to learn more about social entrepreneurship. A deep hunger for knowledge about this field has emerged, and the Center for the Advancement of Social Entrepreneurship (CASE) at Duke University's Fuqua School of Business has led the way in seeking to serve that hunger. The *Social Entrepreneurship Series* represents a new and exciting knowledge dissemination initiative. The series will contain monographs and compendia of papers offering the latest thinking about how to become more effective at social entrepreneurship.

Scaling Social Impact: New Thinking
Edited by Paul N. Bloom and Edward Skloot

Scaling Your Social Venture: Becoming an Impact Entrepreneur
Paul N. Bloom

Scaling Your Social Venture
Becoming an Impact Entrepreneur

Paul N. Bloom

SCALING YOUR SOCIAL VENTURE
Copyright © Paul N. Bloom, 2012.

First published in 2012 by
PALGRAVE MACMILLAN®
in the United States—a division of St. Martin's Press LLC,
175 Fifth Avenue, New York, NY 10010.

Where this book is distributed in the UK, Europe and the rest of the world,
this is by Palgrave Macmillan, a division of Macmillan Publishers Limited,
registered in England, company number 785998, of Houndmills,
Basingstoke, Hampshire RG21 6XS.

Palgrave Macmillan is the global academic imprint of the above companies
and has companies and representatives throughout the world.

Palgrave® and Macmillan® are registered trademarks in the United States,
the United Kingdom, Europe and other countries.

ISBN: 978–0–230–37728–8

Library of Congress Cataloging-in-Publication Data

Bloom, Paul N.
    Scaling your social venture : becoming an impact entrepreneur /
by Paul N. Bloom.
    p. cm.
    ISBN 978–0–230–37728–8
    1. Social entrepreneurship. 2. Scaling (Social sciences) 3. Small
business—Growth. I. Title.

HD60.B58 2012
361.7′65068—dc23   2012000407

A catalogue record of the book is available from the British Library.

Design by Newgen Imaging Systems (P) Ltd., Chennai, India.

First edition: July 2012

10 9 8 7 6 5 4 3 2 1

Printed in the United States of America.

To Shelly

Contents

Illustrations

Figures

Exhibit

Preface

The idea of developing a scaling model to help guide social entrepreneurs came to me a few years ago while reading the best-selling book, *Made to Stick*, written by the brothers Chip and Dan Heath.[1] Among other things, they point out that acronyms can help ideas catch on and be remembered. I thought of my home discipline of marketing, a subject I taught for years and years, and how it has used the device of the "4P's" (standing for Product, Price, Place, and Promotion) to help students remember the essence of marketing. It occurred to me that the emerging field of social entrepreneurship needed a similar "hook" to help students and practitioners understand what it was all about.

As a newcomer to social entrepreneurship, I was struck by how possessed everyone was with the concept of "scaling." Indeed, I have come to believe that more than anything else, what distinguishes social entrepreneurs from more conventional leaders of social-purpose organizations is the former groups' obsession with scaling social impact. These folks want to change the world, not just run a sustainable and effective do-gooder organization. So whatever acronym or words I generated to help the field "stick" had to relate to the concept of scaling.

Fortunately, I was able to use the letters of the acronym SCALERS to refer to what I was detecting from my own research and the research of others as being the organizational capabilities that were the key drivers of successful scaling (i.e., staffing, communicating, alliance-building, lobbying, earnings-generation, replicating, and stimulating market forces). I am very pleased by all the positive feedback and attention my original writing on the model has received.[2]

Still, my thinking about scaling is evolving, and there are aspects of the SCALERS model that I have modified since the earlier articles were published. This book presents this revised thinking. New concepts and ideas are layered onto the original model, and numerous examples are offered to help explain all these notions.

I am grateful to several people for their support of this writing effort. My colleagues at the Center for the Advancement of Social Entrepreneurship at Duke University's Fuqua School have helped me refine my thinking about scaling, while also encouraging me to put my thoughts into the form of a book. Greg Dees, the founder of our center, introduced me to the field of social entrepreneurship when he hired me in 2006 to fill a position on one of his grant projects, and I am still learning a great deal from him. The rest of our center's current team consisting of Cathy Clark, Matt Nash, Erin Worsham, and Ruth Tolman—in addition to former team members Beth Anderson and Wendy Kuran—have provided helpful feedback on my writing and are constantly feeding new ideas to me. I have also benefited from interactions with my Duke colleagues, Ed Skloot and Joel Fleishman, at the Sanford School of Public Policy, as well as from my Fuqua colleague, Ronnie Chatterji, who coauthored the first article on SCALERS with me. Brett Smith of Miami University in Ohio has also been a valued coauthor on some of my previous writing about SCALERS.

Additionally, the editorial support of Laurie Harting of Palgrave Macmillan has been outstanding.

My son, Jonathan Bloom, has influenced my thinking too. He is a TV journalist in San Francisco, and I marvel at his ability to craft visually and verbally compelling and easy-to-understand two-minute stories, often on very complex topics, almost every single night. I have tried very hard to make the contents of this book compelling and easy-to-understand, avoiding academic jargon and convoluted explanations as much as possible.

Finally, I want to say how much I appreciate the fantastic support I have received from my wife, Rochelle (Shelly) Schwartz-Bloom. Shelly is a social entrepreneur herself, trying to change the world by improving science literacy throughout the population, so that people understand what harm they are doing to themselves when they use drugs and alcohol inappropriately. In her role as Director of the Duke Center for Science Education, she has allowed me to witness first-hand the ingenuity and drive that social entrepreneurs have to deploy in order to have social impact. She has been a great sounding board for the ideas in this book, and she has never stopped encouraging me to complete it. I am thrilled to dedicate it to her.

Introduction

Sca.ling: verb. Achieving more efficient and effective adoption of your innovation.

Scaling has become the business-school buzzword of the twenty-first century. Take any venture that is promoting an innovative approach to serving customers or solving social problems, and you will find nearly everyone associated with it focused on scaling. Whether you are talking about investors, funders, suppliers, managers, or employees, they all want their venture to be the next McDonald's, Walmart, Google, or Apple—or, in the social sector, the next Habitat for Humanity, Teach for America, BRAC, or Mothers Against Drunk Driving. As the definition above suggests, getting a huge bang for the bucks invested is what it is all about. Few people are content with doing modestly well (and/or good) while serving only small numbers in a limited geographic region. Most want to take the funds invested by venture capitalists, angel investors, impact investors, foundations, governments, or small donors and hit it out of the park, becoming an international success story and solving lots of social problems in a sustainable, efficient way.

The obsession with scaling appears everywhere, from the pages of major business magazines to the annual reports of venture capitalists to the business plans created by entrepreneurs to the missions of government programs like the Social Innovation Fund in the United States that wants to scale-up effective solutions to social problems. Indeed, in announcing the formation of the Fund, First Lady Michelle Obama demonstrated that she and the president have bought into the idea of scaling by stating that the Fund was formed "to help innovative nonprofit groups and social entrepreneurs... expand their successful approaches to tackling our most pressing national challenges. The idea is simple: find the most effective programs out there and then provide the capital needed to replicate their success in communities around the country.[1]"

With so much attention paid to scaling in recent years, it is tempting to see it as something that has only recently been discovered as a challenge, making it ripe for finding a new secret sauce for success. There are those who believe that all you need to do is gather a lot of smart, experienced people together who have had varying degrees of success at getting innovations adopted, and that they will collaboratively identify the truths about what works for scaling. Thus, the Social Innovation Fund is trying to establish "learning communities" that will allow people to figure out what "works." But the challenge of scaling is not new, and many businesses and nonprofits have struggled mightily for years with how to accomplish it.

Indeed, the major theme of this book is that scaling is extremely difficult; the approaches that will work for one organization in one situation will not necessarily work for another organization in only a slightly different situation. I argue that scaling success requires enormously disciplined research, hard work, and creativity, and it is not something that can be accomplished merely by throwing a lot of money at a venture and setting up metrics and milestones to make sure that the originally conceived and potentially shortsighted plan is executed properly. The ecosystem in which the venture operates must be fully understood, and strategies must be planned, executed, and adapted to build organizational capabilities in seven areas, which you can remember by using the acronym SCALERS: staffing, communicating, alliance-building, lobbying, earnings-generation, replicating, and stimulating Market Forces.

I first became aware of how much passion people have for scaling while writing a thesis for my MBA degree at The Wharton School of the University of Pennsylvania in the late 1960s. My topic was suggested to me by one of the Pennsylvania state legislators, whom I consulted to try to identify an issue that involved both marketing and finance, which were my dual majors, and that also had some social welfare and public policy aspects to it. The social impact of business decisions has always been of great interest to me. The legislator turned me on to "Dutch Chicken" and "White Whale," two prototype restaurants that had been opened near the state capital in Harrisburg, touted as the second comings of Kentucky Fried Chicken and Arthur Treacher's Fish and Chips. My thesis became a case study of why these ventures failed to scale and subsequently went bankrupt, disrupting the lives of hundreds of people.

The founders of these ventures claimed that if they could get enough investors to buy shares in the franchisor companies, they would then have the base funding they needed to scale up their ventures through selling franchises all over the country. Unfortunately, hundreds of people bought shares in these franchisors, even though the branding and marketing were suspect, financing for the franchisees was going to be difficult to arrange, and the social benefits of having two more fast-food chains littering the landscape were questionable. The lure of scaling—hoping to become part of the next McDonald's—was just too much for investors to resist. Many people lost a lot of money on these deals because nobody dug in and figured out what it would take for scaling to occur with these ventures.

I fear that many of today's heavily promoted new ventures will turn out to be Dutch Chickens or White Whales, because too many entrepreneurs are unwilling or unable to do the incredibly hard work needed for scaling success. They may think that a clever brand name and a shiny new prototype, with a well-written and presented business plan or prospectus, are all they need. However, successful scaling takes so much more than this.

I especially worry about social entrepreneurs becoming Dutch Chickens and White Whales. Innovators in the social sector often do not have the same capability of harnessing financial incentives to help them scale. I have been a business school professor long enough to see a small enterprise become a major international brand in 10 years' time, namely, Apple, eBay, Amazon, Google, Best Buy, and Costco, to name a few. Yet I have not seen anything even remotely close to this kind of scaling by social purpose organizations because they simply cannot put financial incentives to work in the same way. Even the recent darling of social entrepreneurship, the microfinance industry, has found there are limits to how much they can rely on financial incentives to fuel their growth and mission of social impact.

For the purposes of this book, I will focus on scaling for social entrepreneurs, not on scaling for entrepreneurs more generally. That doesn't mean I won't identify insights learned from business entrepreneurs that have great relevance to social entrepreneurs. And, conversely, that doesn't mean that the insights offered here about scaling for social entrepreneurs are not of relevance to more conventional business entrepreneurs. But I believe social entrepreneurs face much bigger obstacles, and they are in much greater need of new thinking about whether and how to scale.

This book will also focus on scaling social impact, and not just on scaling the size of the social entrepreneurial organization. There will be situations where the size is a prerequisite for achieving social impact, but there are other situations where social impact can be accomplished without growing an organization. Even small, nongrowing organizations can achieve great social impact through approaches like mounting a highly persuasive communications campaign or pursuing a successful lawsuit. In a sense, they can scale deep instead of wide. Hence, the definition of scaling social impact used here is: the process of closing the gap between the real and ideal conditions as they pertain to particular social needs or problems.[2]

The primary audience I hope to reach with this book is practicing and would-be social entrepreneurs: leaders of a venture that employs innovative approaches to address social problems. The innovations can emerge in the ways the venture's products or services function, the ways they are distributed and delivered, the advocacy approach of the venture, the ways the venture accumulates and deploys financial, human, and other resources, or the ways its networks or partnerships are configured. The venture can reside within a nonprofit, for-profit, hybrid, or government organization, and it can certainly seek goals that involve generating financial surpluses, but achieving social impact must be one of its primary goals for the label social entrepreneur to apply.

To get started, the introduction of the book will address the important basic question: when does it make sense to try to scale a social entrepreneurial venture? This will be followed by a chapter that lays out what the scaling-seeking social entrepreneur should try to understand about the ecosystem in which he or she operates in order to maximize chances for success. Next, a separate chapter is devoted to each of the SCALERS, with thoughts provided about how each of these organizational capabilities can be configured to contribute maximally to effective scaling. Finally, the concluding chapter offers some final words of encouragement and guidance for those who want to persevere and take on the challenge of scaling. A step-by-step approach is suggested for assessing the organization's unique situation and interpreting what that situation implies for determining the most effective strategies for scaling impact. Recognition is given to the fact that what would be a strong scaling strategy for one organization at a certain stage in its history may be at totally inappropriate strategy at another stage in its life cycle. This final chapter contains a set of questions that can be used to do a self-assessment of an organization's scaling approach.

CHAPTER 1

On Your Mark, Get Set, Scale?

The first time I entered a triathlon, in 1991, I ended up losing my way during the opening swim, crossing the rope in the lake that divided outgoing from incoming swimmers, and actually swimming head-on into the top swimmers, who were finishing their lap and returning to shore as I was very slowly trying to make my way away from the starting point. I was so humiliated that I quit the race. A year later, I entered the same race and didn't get lost at the swim start—but I had an enormous panic attack and quit the swim after two minutes. I did the biking and running part anyway, but couldn't consider myself an official finisher. These were short triathlons (half-mile swim, 15-mile bike, 5K run), and I thought I could handle them based on my background as a 10K and half-marathon runner, but I was wrong.

The next time I tried something new and a bit imposing was when I entered my first 26.2-mile marathon in 1998. I figured I would be OK if I kept everything on dry land. Yet that was a disaster too. I ended up dropping out at mile 23 with terrible blisters on my feet that took weeks to heal. To be honest, I simply was not ready for the challenges these races represented.

I had not acquired the resources and capabilities necessary to complete these events successfully.

With the end of the year 2011, I have now completed 16 marathons and hundreds of triathlons, including 12 half-iron man races (1.2-mile swim, 56-mile bike, and 13.1-mile run). I have systematically acquired the resources and capabilities needed to successfully complete the challenges of marathons and triathlons. I won't start a triathlon without certain resources or assets like a fit and healthy body, a comfortable wetsuit (if the water is cold), swim goggles that don't leak, a well-tuned bicycle, bicycle shoes and running shoes that are easy to put on, sunglasses, suntan lotion, Body Glide (to avoid chafing and blisters), and loads of drinks, food, and electrolyte pills to consume during the race. In my training for a race, I make sure that I have practiced hard and developed capabilities or competences in swimming under crowded conditions, biking up and down steep hills, and eating while competing.

Similarly, before social entrepreneurs attempt to grow and scale they also need to be ready with the necessary resources and capabilities. Just like an athlete must have his or her body fit and healthy to attempt a new challenge, a social entrepreneur must have a sound and healthy program or idea that is poised to be rolled out, not something that is shaky or untested. The program or idea must have a well-thought-out "theory of change" (or "logic model"), and the validity of that theory must have at least been demonstrated in a small and more controlled setting. Thus, for example, an innovative educational intervention must already be improving test scores and keeping kids in school in the places where it has already been tried, and a new health intervention must already be improving health outcomes at a low cost where it has been implemented.

Theory of Change

The way to specify your organization's theory of change (i.e., logic model) is to think deeply about the actions or initiatives you are trying to implement and the effects, outcomes, and impacts that you want to achieve as a result of what you are doing.[1] What are the causal linkages that you are creating? If you have an innovative job-training program, is it leading to the participants staying in the program, acquiring jobs when graduating, and, in turn, improving the quality of their lives? Is the neighborhood that is served by the program experiencing lower crime rates and reduced use of drugs and alcohol? Mapping out desired causes and effects in a chart or diagram that specifies inputs, activities, outputs, outcomes, and impacts is helpful for thinking through an initiative.

Figure 1.1 presents a mapping of the theory of change for a program that promotes fair-trade chocolate. The diagram hypothesizes that the establishment of a trustworthy inspection and monitoring program (input), followed by inspections (activities) that certify that fair-trade principles are being followed at cacao plantations (i.e., fair wages, fair treatment of workers, fair returns to landowners, sustainable farming practices), along with promotion of the fair-trade concept to multiple parties, will lead to the greater availability of fair-trade chocolate products for retail sales (outputs) and more consumers wanting to patronize brands of chocolate that have the certification (outcomes). This will feed back to greater sales for certified brands than alternative brands, which should lead plantation owners to want to participate in certification programs (additional outcomes). This should then result in steadier financial returns to the plantations and more predictable incomes for the plantation workers, helping them escape poverty and contributing to the economic revitalization of

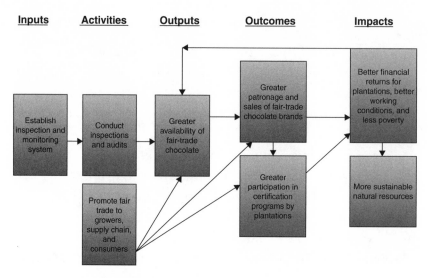

Figure 1.1   Logic Model for a Fair-Trade Chocolate Program

their communities (impacts). It should also help the sustainability of the natural resources in the communities (additional impacts).

Another example of a theory of change comes from WINGS for Kids, a social venture in Charleston, South Carolina, which has developed an after-school program for disadvantaged elementary-school children that strives to improve their social and emotional health. WINGS recently was designated the winner of the 2011 Social Impact Exchange Business Plan Competition for early-stage ventures. WINGS won the award because they demonstrated that they had laid the groundwork necessary to grow outside of their local outreach, including articulating the following theory of change: "Kids receive a comprehensive social and emotional education within an after school program of two years or more → they develop high social and emotional skills → they demonstrate good behavior and a high attachment to school → they graduate from high school, stay out of jail, and avoid teenage parenthood → they have a good chance of success and happiness."[2]

Other theories of change start with different inputs/activities and produce different causal chains. The theory of change for a social venture capitalist might begin with raising a large amount of financial capital for a social cause, which in turn can lead to greater capacity for certain ventures to serve people and generate revenue while doing so. If more people are served in a financially sustainable way, improvements could occur in outcomes involving health, education, or welfare, and this could eventually lead to the alleviation of poverty, lower disparity of income, and less social tension. In a similar vein, a theory of change could start with setting up a distribution system for a new medical device, drug, vaccine, or diagnostic test. Wider distribution could eventually produce significant health improvements and better quality of life. Note that some theories may involve scaling the size of the social entrepreneurial organization, while other theories will hypothesize that scaling social impact can occur without organizational growth.

Evidence of Effectiveness

Once your theory of change has been mapped, you then need to search for objective evidence that the positive effects that seem to be materializing from your initiatives are clearly the result of your actions and not the result of everything else in the world. This can be extremely difficult and potentially expensive, but unless you have this evidence—especially in today's world of philanthropy and social investing—you are not going to get very far in persuading providers of financial capital to support you. In hard economic times, investors need to feel very confident in your ability to measure success. Investors who participate in social entrepreneurship want to believe in the mission and the cause, but they also need to be able to make a calculated decision about where to invest. They want to know they are siding with documented potential winners.

Jordan Kassalow, the founder and leader of VisionSpring, an organization that distributes and sells very inexpensive reading glasses in developing countries (and is now expanding into other eye-care services) attributes much of his ability to attract financial resources for growth from foundations and donors to a positive evaluation study of his efforts by a group from the University of Michigan. In an article he wrote about his experiences with the Michigan group, Kassalow states:

> VisionSpring partnered with University of Michigan's William Davidson Institute from 2005 to 2010 to study the impact VisionSpring eyeglasses have on low-income populations in the developing world. The goal was to determine if there is a link between correcting presbyopia, the form of blurry vision that occurs as the eyes age and is easily corrected with reading glasses, and economic capacity. Analysis of the data demonstrated there is a direct relationship between the use of eyeglasses among those with presbyopia and an increased ability to work as well as tangible gains in income. The University of Michigan team found that customers wearing reading glasses reported 35% higher productivity as compared to those who did not correct their vision. Further analysis by the VisionSpring team uncovered that the use of reading glasses results in a 20% gain in monthly income. Based on this significant research, VisionSpring created a social impact measure to understand the economic impact of using our reading glasses. Multiplying conservative estimates of average daily income, working days per year, and expected life of a pair of eyeglasses, VisionSpring calculates that each pair of glasses produces at least $381 in increased earning potential over two years, for each of our target customers. With over 600,000 eyeglasses sold, VisionSpring has generated an astounding $228 million in economic growth at the Base of the Pyramid.[3]

Similarly, WINGS for Kids was helped in its quest for awards and financial capital by studies that showed that "students enrolled in WINGS demonstrate significantly higher math and reading scores, grades, and school attendance when compared to non-WINGS students. Additional metrics report WINGS students have higher self-esteem, less anxiety, and greater satisfaction with school than non-WINGS kids. The organization's own data shows WINGS kids graduate at a rate 40% higher than their peers who did not receive WINGS."[4]

Evaluation Research Methods

How do you gather hard evidence that will persuade others that your business plan will be successful in multiple environments? The gold standard for creating this evidence is the "randomized controlled trial," which involves conducting research that parallels what is done in testing the safety and efficacy of a new drug. An "experimental" group uses the new drug, and a "control" group does not (or uses a previously approved drug that has become the "standard" level of care for an ailment), and a random draw is conducted to determine who receives the new drug and who becomes part of a control group. If there are differences in the outcomes achieved by the experimental group compared to the control group, it becomes appropriate to attribute those outcomes to the drug, since the two groups, if sufficient in sample size, should be basically the same because of the random assignment, other than having received different drug treatment.

Consulting organizations such as Innovations for Poverty Action (see www.poverty-action.org) have used randomized controlled trials to evaluate microfinance initiatives and health interventions. For example, a study was conducted in Kenya on the benefits of distributing chlorine dispensers to communities so that people can treat their water at communal water sources, protecting them from waterborne illnesses. When communities were randomly assigned to treatment with a promoter and a community dispenser, take-up was approximately 40 percent in the short term (3 weeks), but climbed to more than 60 percent by the medium term (3 to 6 months), representing 37- and 53-percentage-point gains, respectively, over the control group.[5]

Unfortunately, randomized controlled trials can be very expensive and difficult to administer. Purely random assignment of individuals to groups, as is done in drug trials, may not be practical when an intervention is implemented in a community setting (like the water treatment example) or a classroom setting—and one can only randomly assign communities or teachers to different interventions. In these cases, community or teacher effects on outcomes must be controlled for in the analysis, and even when this is done carefully, the results may not be as unambiguous as they are with random assignment of individuals. Furthermore, randomized controlled trials can raise ethical issues. It may be unethical or discriminatory to give some people the privilege of receiving a social intervention while withholding that intervention from others.

Still, some type of random assignment is better than trying to obtain what are known as "counterfactuals" by doing things like finding "matching" groups or by looking at before-and-after data on the same individuals or groups. One way to achieve random assignment without running into problems of withholding interventions can occur when you have an over-supply of demand for your intervention. Random assignment can be used to put people into an intervention group and a "wait-list" control group, with the after scores of the first group being compared to the before scores of the second group (who will still get the intervention, but later than the first group). This kind of design has worked well with oversubscribed educational and health interventions. For example, my wife, who creates educational modules designed to improve science literacy among young people, has used this approach. A large number of schools and teachers sought to use her modules, which teach students about drugs of abuse as a way to engage them in learning basic biology and chemistry concepts. Yet, instead of giving all the schools the modules, she randomly assigned half of them to receive the modules in year 1 of an evaluation and the other half in year 2 (who were controls in year 1). By comparing these two reasonably equivalent sets of schools (and students) after year 1, she was able to establish that the modules helped students learn basic biology and chemistry concepts significantly better than the standard material that was being used and that the more modules they used (up to four), the greater the effects (i.e., a dose-response effect).[6]

Of course, as indicated, trying to do some type of random assignment, along with sophisticated data analysis that controls for potential confounding factors, can make obtaining evaluation data very expensive. You have to pay talented people for their time to design the studies and conduct the analyses, and you have to pay both to collect the data and monitor that all the interventions and procedures are introduced in a uniform and accurate manner. Indeed, determining which metrics will accurately measure desired outcomes and impacts creates further challenges and expenses.

Although funders use these kinds of data and results to help evaluate the likelihood of success, if you don't have the money to perform these randomized controlled trials, you still must do what you can to evaluate the initiative you are thinking of scaling. You don't want the perfect to be the enemy of the good. If the effects that are discovered through the use of less rigorous methods are large, there is nothing wrong in putting some faith in less expensive studies that try to do matching of groups with similar profiles, with one receiving the intervention and the other not, or that look at before-after changes.

World Bicycle Relief has used both of these alternative approaches to evaluate their programs that distribute basic, functional bicycles in poor African countries. For example, they conducted one study comparing two matched districts of the northern province of Zambia: Mpika and Mbala. Bicycles were given out to caregivers of human immunodeficiency virus/ acquired immune deficiency syndrome (HIV/AIDS) patients and to households headed by youth in Mpika, with Mbala serving as a control for the eight-month study. Results indicated that caregivers could thus serve more people and were more likely to continue in this role, while youths were more likely to attend school.[7] And in another study, they tracked school attendance over time in five schools in Zambia where all students received bikes, finding that school attendance improved from 68 percent to 90 percent in a four-month period.[8]

Another approach involves comparing what your initiative has done to what "average" initiatives by other organizations are reported to have accomplished. Foundations and funders can sometimes supply information about what comparable organizations have achieved. Combining data acquired by using these less rigorous methods along with qualitative information with narratives or anecdotes about the positive effects of an intervention can give you the confidence that you know whether it is worthwhile to try to scale or not. There is a rich literature on evaluation research methods that can be consulted for further ideas.[9]

Minimal Resources and Capabilities for Scaling

Assuming you have reasonable evidence that your theory of change can work, you must consider whether you are starting your scaling effort with the minimal resources and capabilities required to launch a serious attempt to replicate the initial success. You need to assess your human, social, political, financial, technological, and natural-resource capital, as well as your access to key markets, to see if shortcomings in any of these areas will make a scaling launch highly risky. You also need to consider each of the seven SCALERS (i.e., Staffing, Communicating, etc.) and judge whether these organizational capabilities already exist or have a good likelihood of being developed. This means taking a first pass at the ecosystem analysis introduced in the next chapter. A deeper dive into the ecosystem will be necessary once you decide to get serious about growth, but to make a go-no-go decision you need to have a heart-to-heart with yourself about whether your gut tells you that you have enough resources and capabilities to commence.

These questions about resources should be considered carefully:

- Do you have a good group of people already working with you in staff positions, management, and on your board, and do you only need to add people in proportion to how much you grow, or are your current human resources stretched and overcommitted? (human capital)
- Are you known in the community and capable of marshaling support for your initiatives pretty easily, or are most people totally unaware of what you do? (social capital)
- Have you avoided involvement with something politically controversial (e.g., abortion) that would make it difficult to obtain government support and funding? (political capital)
- Are there discretionary funds available that can be reallocated to new initiatives, or are you constantly scrounging for money and unsure about how you will pay the next month's bills? (financial capital)
- Do you have the computer systems, telecommunications systems, and data-base management systems needed to support your initiatives in an efficient and effective manner? (technological capital)

- Do you have access to the natural resources needed to carry out your initiatives? (natural-resource capital)
- Do you have access to markets where you would like to become an exchange participant? (access to markets)

And these questions about organizational capabilities should be considered carefully:

- Can you become effective at recruiting, training, organizing, managing, and retaining the additional employees, managers, volunteers, and board members needed to support scaling? (staffing)
- Can you become effective at configuring and delivering messages that persuade potential donors, employees, volunteers, partners, regulators, and beneficiaries about the social value of what you do? (communicating)
- Can you become effective at forming partnerships and alliances with other parties and organizations that will allow you to leverage their resources and capabilities in addition to your own? (alliance-building)
- Can you become effective at advocating with influential people and public policy makers for the social changes you seek? (lobbying)
- Can you develop a business model that will allow you to be financially sustainable? (earnings-generation)
- Can you become effective at developing systems and procedures that facilitate replicating or repeating your successful interventions? (replicating)
- Can you become effective at using market incentives to encourage others to donate, buy, invest, volunteer, or otherwise behave in ways that benefit your venture? (stimulating market forces)

Positive answers to the bulk of these questions will help you convince yourself that scaling is feasible, although admittedly the answers to these questions may depend on your theory of change. For example, you would be more likely to appraise your human capital and staffing as being sufficient if your change strategy did not involve the deployment of labor-intensive services. So you need to assess the interplay between your theory of change and your starting resources and capabilities before moving ahead.

Business Model for Scaling

While all the questions raised above require serious consideration before you attempt to scale, it is especially important to consider your capability of developing a financially sustainable business model. How will money flow as your operation develops? How sensitive will that flow be to adjustments in your theory of change or shifts in the suppliers, distributors, partners, customers, and beneficiaries with whom you interact? Not all of this has to be figured out completely before you start—since developing the Earnings-Generation capability is something that can be pursued as you proceed and as you learn more about the financial implications of all your actions. But you need to acquire some strong sense of the business model—or the financial inflows and outflows created by your actions and relationships—before trying to take off. The temptation to believe that "the money thing always works itself out" often turns out to be a false promise that many social entrepreneurs accept too readily. They neglect information like the fact that one-third of all Echoing Green social entrepreneur fellows—selected for a two-year $80,000 fellowship after considerable due diligence has been done on them and their "early-stage" ideas—never reach financial sustainability, and 42 percent don't reach overall budgets of $100,000 during the two years after receiving the award.[10]

A business plan with pro forma projections of revenues, expenses, loan amounts, cash flows, income statements, and balance sheets is essential, even if many of the numbers that are entered are little more than "educated guesses." Where the most difficult estimates that will occur for most organizations will be the projected sources of revenues, these are also the most important.

Before attempting to scale, the organization should have a high level of confidence that it can meet a certain percentage of its revenue needs from foundation grants, another percent from government grants, still another percent from donations, and finally another percent from earned-income ventures, with the total at least matching projected expenses for the planning horizon. Moreover, contingency plans for turning to alternative business models should be developed. What will you do if your original projection of being able to generate 50 percent of your operating expenses through an earned-income venture selling crafts produced by poor Indian women turns out to be overly optimistic? Do you have a Plan B involving another earned-income venture selling organic, fair-trade food products? Or is there a government agency somewhere that might provide funding, given that by that time you feel you will have hard evidence from a rigorous evaluation that your innovative health intervention really saves lives? If your health intervention isn't adopted as widely as you hoped through word-of-mouth referrals and much more money needs to be spent on advertising and marketing to create awareness and interest in the intervention, are there major corporations that you plan to approach to help you with this advertising and marketing, perhaps as part of one of their corporate social responsibility initiatives? The more you think through these money-flow contingencies before attempting to scale, the lower the risks will become of a "go" decision.

An example of an organization that has considered its business model is the Greater Boston Food Bank (GBFB), the largest hunger-relief organization in New England. This organization distributes nearly 35 million pounds of food annually to more than 600 local organizations, including food pantries, soup kitchens, day-care centers, senior centers, and homeless shelters. Over 16,000 volunteers per year help to sort and distribute donated food. GBFB acquires goods in many ways. The dominant sources of goods are retailers and manufacturers. It also receives surplus food from restaurants and hotels. In 2006, corporate in-kind support accounted for 52 percent of GBFB's revenues. Federal and state government programs provide GBFB with in-kind goods and money, accounting for 23 percent of its annual budget, which GBFB uses to purchase food for distribution. Cash donations from individuals make up the remaining 25 percent of revenues, covering overhead and capital improvements. While these percentages have shifted somewhat with the recent recession, the organization has continued to grow and serve its very needy beneficiaries efficiently and effectively.[11]

Saying "No" to Scaling

Clearly, many social entrepreneurial organizations will go through the self-analysis just described and determine that they lack the evidence of effectiveness, the resources, or the capabilities to be ready for scaling and should hold off or back off from any early scaling attempts. And some will determine that although they seem to be ready to scale, they just don't have the motivation to pursue such an all-consuming effort.

Recent history is filled with many examples of organizations that were very successful in operating on a small scale, but that held back trying to scale for as long as decades because they did not feel they had the evidence, resources, and capabilities to support scaling. Well-known operations like Bill Strickland's Manchester Bidwell Corporation in Pittsburgh and Paul Farmer's Partners in Health in Haiti really did not make serious attempts to scale until they were well established in a limited geographic market. Although Strickland had a very effective job-training program he started in 1968, which was financially sustainable when operating only in Pittsburgh, the human and financial resources needed to scale did not appear to be there until 2003, when replication attempts were commenced through a new National Center for Arts and Technology.[12] And Farmer's treatment program for infectious diseases like HIV/AIDS and tuberculosis (TB) began saving lives in Haiti in 1987 and moved on to Peru in 1994, but it was not rolled out to Russia and Africa until after the year 2000, when the human, financial, and technological resources needed for maintaining quality control in health-care delivery in these other localities could be accumulated.[13]

More recent examples of initiatives not feeling ready to scale can be found in Libraries Across Africa, Fenix International, and Coach for College. At this writing, all three of these organizations have launched programs that have accumulated seed funding or won competitions, but they have held off on serious growth efforts until they feel more comfortable with their scaling strategies. Libraries Across Africa seeks to empower Africans and improve their lives through providing reading material, Internet access, and technology training at new modular-designed libraries that also serve as community centers. Their first library is being built in Ghana, and they hope to generate revenues and contribute to sustainability in a number of ways, such as charging for Internet access and printing and also renting out the building for events.[14]

Fenix International has developed the ReadySet battery that can be charged by a mini-solar panel or by riding a stationary bicycle. It can provide a relatively low-cost source of power for lighting, charging cell phones, or running other electrical devices, bringing many modern conveniences to the developing world. Besides generating revenue by selling these batteries (along with the panels) in poor regions, Fenix also hopes to sell the product as an emergency generator at a higher price point in developed countries, potentially cross-subsidizing the scaling efforts in less developed countries.[15]

Coach for College brings US intercollegiate athletes to Vietnam for three-week summer sessions that teach middle-school children about sports, study habits, and potential college opportunities. The idea is to leverage sports to encourage Vietnamese youth to think about college as a possibility, while at the same time encouraging the US athletes to think about new types of career paths in education and development. Thus far, support has come from the sports programs and general funds of the universities that have sent athlete/coaches, with additional support from athletic equipment suppliers. They see involvement with this program as providing enhancement to their institutional reputations. The hope is that more schools and companies will see the value to themselves of providing this financial support.[16]

All three of these programs have held back from scaling because they feel they lack "proof of concept." They have yet to acquire the solid evaluation studies showing they have had social impact, and they have not shown that they have a business model that can achieve financial sustainability without a large and continuous flow of philanthropic funds.

An example of an organization that actually tried to scale rapidly and then realized it needed to say "no" to its original scaling approach is Progreso Financiero, a bank based in

Mountain View, California. It offers small loans, averaging $1,000, to individuals and small businesses with little or no credit history, through staffed kiosks in Hispanic grocery stores and pharmacies in California and Texas. Borrowers often use the loans to buy a delivery truck or other equipment. Started in 2005 by James Gutierrez, a graduate of Stanford University's Masters of Business Administration program, they originally offered the loans at kiosks in Sears and Kmart stores, seeing the ties with those chains as a potential path to rapid scaling. But Sears and Kmart gave up on Progreso because loan volume was too low, and Gutierrez realized he had to refocus on basic building blocks like technology, automated credit scoring, and the use of neighborhood stores. Not going full speed ahead with a flawed expansion plan proved to be a blessing for Gutierrez, and following the retrenchment, he has secured more than $75 million in venture capital and another $75 million in debt financing, allowing Progresso to issue more than 160,000 loans in the last few years. The bank is expected to become profitable in 2012.[17]

As for organizations that feel that they might be able to scale effectively, but choose not to do so because they are content with having a smaller-scale but meaningful impact in their original communities, the examples of The SEED School in Washington, DC, and TROSA in Durham, North Carolina, come to mind. The SEED School has received recognition for getting 95 percent of its first six classes to enroll in colleges within 18 months of graduation. It is the United States' first urban public boarding school, which now serves approximately 400 students, with admission determined through a lottery. The school appears to be able to stay solvent, yet their founders are satisfied with continuing to serve Washington, DC, children and not getting involved with scaling their programs through developing new branches or franchising, unlike other charter school systems like Knowledge Is Power Program (KIPP), Lighthouse Academies, or Uncommon Schools.[18]

TROSA (Triangle Residential Options for Substance Abusers) in Durham, North Carolina, has created a two-year residential program that helps substance abusers get clean, advances their educational credentials, and teaches them job skills through offering them positions in the highly successful moving, landscaping, used-furniture, and Christmas-tree businesses that are run to finance the operation. One-hundred percent of their graduates leave TROSA with a job in the community. Kevin McDonald, TROSA's founder and leader, recognizes that others could replicate much of what he does—after all, he started TROSA by copying many of the things done by Delancey Street Foundation in San Francisco—yet he is not interested in leading a scaling effort.[19]

Saying "Yes" to Scaling: JUMP Math

An organization that has thought through all the issues raised in this chapter—and now seems ready to mount a substantial scaling effort—is JUMP Math.[20] JUMP is an acronym for Junior Undiscovered Math Prodigies. This organization was started in 1999 by John Mighton, who received a PhD in mathematics from the University of Toronto and went on to develop a mathematics curriculum that is now being used throughout Canada and parts of England, transforming the way math is taught to children of all ability levels. Mighton's venture received an early boost when he was named an Ashoka Fellow, which provided him with significant funding and access to Ashoka's support network, which he is still taking advantage of for help with scaling (see below). Ashoka is one of the major organizations that honors, supports, and assists social entrepreneurs. Others include the Skoll Foundation, Echoing Green, the Schwab Foundation, the Draper-Richards Foundation, and Civic Ventures. Being recognized by any of these award grantors is often an indicator that the organization is ready to scale, since the criteria these grantors use to select awardees tend to be similar to the criteria mentioned in this chapter.

The JUMP Math program's philosophy involves teaching math concepts in very small bite-sized pieces—not relying on rote memorization of how numbers combine or "problem-based learning"—and allowing children to build their confidence with explicit guidance and frequent practice sessions as they move step-by-step from the simplest concepts to more complex ones. The concepts are also taught to children using simple contexts that enhance motivation and learning, such as tending to animals and insects or telling time.

The organization's website contains a lengthy description of the research that has guided the development of the curriculum, and they have built on insights that look to:

- Provide students with regular confidence-building exercises that look challenging but enable all students to do well
- Review basic skills and concepts thoroughly before introducing new topics, so all students can start on an equal footing, and target less confident students with special "bonus" questions that allow them to experience success. When students feel equally capable, their brains work efficiently, and they tend to become equally capable.
- Give students problems that become incrementally harder to show them they can surmount any challenge through their work. Students learn best when they are allowed to take moderate risks with positive feedback.
- Practice doesn't need to be "drill and kill." Turn practice into games that engage students and make math

enjoyable, by embedding it in exercises in which students are challenged, constantly reach higher levels of success, and receive immediate feedback.

- Minimize the use of text in student materials, and introduce language gradually and rigorously. Place activities or exercises that require lengthy descriptions in the teacher's guides. Ask students to communicate their understanding, but allow pictures, numbers, or oral answers when writing is a challenge.
- Use "guided discovery" to teach for deep understanding: deliver lessons in well-scaffolded steps, so one concept naturally leads to the next and students have enough practice to master the concepts, but let students discover the connections between ideas themselves as much as possible.[21]

Thus, the theory of change they are pursuing is that greater use of their JUMP Math books and teacher's guides—as well as a greater deployment of teachers who have been trained at JUMP Math seminars—will allow even weak students to develop good or even excellent math skills, and this should help them perform better in other courses, as well as set them up for other successes in life. The JUMP Math leaders have confidence in the validity of their theory because it is based on the research mentioned above. However, they have also recognized the need to conduct rigorous evaluations of their curriculum, and they have done several studies that have found persuasive evidence that their curriculum does what it is supposed to do. For example:

- A team from Toronto's Hospital for Sick Children, The Ontario Institute for Studies in Education, and the University of Toronto conducted a randomized controlled study that followed 272 students selected from 29 classrooms, in 18 schools, in a rural Canadian school board. Teachers (classes) were randomly assigned to use either JUMP Math or the incumbent math program, and the teachers in each group received equivalent training in the respective programs. Researchers found that the math knowledge of children using JUMP Math grew twice as much as that of children using the incumbent program.[22]

- JUMP Math has worked for several years with the Borough of Lambeth, an inner-city area of London that is the third-neediest borough in England. In 1998, the percentage of children achieving the expected level in mathematics in the Borough trailed the national average by 9 percent (49 percent vs. 58 percent). By 2007, the year that JUMP was introduced in Lambeth, Lambeth's pass rate had risen to 71 percent, but remained 6 percent below the national average. Three years later, Lambeth's year-6 mathematics achievement exceeded the national average by 2 percent. Indeed, they tracked two groups of students who wrote the year-6 national exams in 2009, one of which used JUMP for two years and the other of which used JUMP for one year. Only 12 percent of the first group of 353 struggling students were at or above grade level at the beginning of year-5, and many were several grades behind, yet 60 percent of this group passed the national exams at the end of year-6 (a five-fold rise in pass rates). A second group of 150 students used JUMP for one year. Only 28 percent of these students were at or above grade level at the start of year-6, with many being several grades behind, yet 62 percent passed the year-6 exam. The Borough's year-6 pass rate rose from 6 percent below the national average in 2007 to 2 percent above in 2010. The greater rate of improvement among children who used JUMP Math for two years versus one year, appears to bear out teachers' qualitative assessments that progress with JUMP Math accelerates over time.

- During her first year using JUMP, a Toronto teacher lifted her class average ranking from the sixty-sixth percentile on the grade 5 TOMA test to the ninety-second percentile on the grade 6 test, in September of the following year. Her next class improved its average ranking from the fifty-fourth to the ninety-eighth percentiles. The teacher reported that she followed the JUMP lesson plans more closely with her second class. In both cases, the lowest post-JUMP ranking equaled or exceeded the highest pre-JUMP ranking. In addition, all but one child in each class wrote the Mathematica Pythagoras, and 14 of 17 achieved distinction (the Pythagoras math contest emphasizes problem solving and is written by approximately 5 percent of Canadian grade 6 students—in general, Canada's "top" math students).[23]

The persuasiveness of this evidence has had much to do with JUMP Math's ability to scale to serving more than 65,000 school children and 20,000 home-schooled children across Canada by 2011. However, the organization feels they have only scratched the surface on the number of children they can help in Canada and, beyond that, all over the world. Hence, they have worked to assess whether they have the minimal resources and capabilities needed to start a major scaling effort, beyond having the very important evidence of effectiveness, and it appears that they do. As far as resources go, they possess several key assets. The human capital available is strong, as Mighton is still deeply engaged in the operation and has assembled an enthusiastic, yet small team around him. This is not a program that requires having human resources to deliver services, so the staffing needs will not be as severe as for other organizations. Teachers and parents deliver the services in this situation. JUMP Math mainly needs people to work at refining and writing the curriculum, evaluating it, marketing it, and obtaining donations and grants.

Social capital is another strength, as the teachers and parents that have used the program and seen its results have become advocates and word-of-mouth advertisers. Social capital has also been enhanced through the group's forging alliances with a number of education and funding organizations, including becoming part of the Ashoka Globalizer program. The Globalizer program can provide ideas, benchmarks, and guidance as it pursues its mission to:

- Raise awareness among social entrepreneurs of the full market potential of their ideas.
- Recruit selected Ashoka Fellows to cocreate innovative strategies for globalizing their impact and serve as role models for the field
- Build a community of practice around scaling social impact by enabling structured entrepreneur-to-entrepreneur encounters between these Fellows and a tight community of powerful supporters
- Extract underlying patterns and disseminate these broadly, empowering all social entrepreneurs to develop more effective impact scaling strategies[24]

It appears that the opportunities to achieve networking with Ashoka and others should enhance JUMP Math's ability to scale, especially into markets where Ashoka is well known. JUMP Math's expansion plans include approaching English-speaking countries first, while also approaching French-speaking populations in Canada (and creating French materials). Nevertheless, access to markets may prove troublesome to JUMP Math, as textbook publishers and school systems, committed to other forms of math education and having a large financial stake in maintaining the status quo, could make entry difficult. One way to ease entry would be through developing political capital and then lobbying school boards and school administrators, but this will be hard to do in foreign markets like the United States. This is clearly a place where having strong evaluation data with evidence of effectiveness could make a difference.

The JUMP Math management has also thought through what would be the best business model to deploy for supporting scaling and, as a result, they approach their scaling effort with more financial capital. Mighton recognizes that keeping costs low is an advantage in scaling, and he has stated that:

> Our program is cheaper than other programs. An investment from a corporate partner or a few large donors could in a very short time mean we could reach every school in the country. The gain to our economy and culture would be tremendous.[25]

But Mighton does not want to rely too heavily on grants and donations, even though his organization has managed to obtain significant funding from corporations—especially energy companies and financial institutions—and foundations. He recognizes that JUMP Math can become an operation that can support a high percentage of its budget through earned-income activities. There is the potential for great financial payoffs from selling their books and guides and also providing training and consulting to school systems. The nonprofit or charity status of JUMP Math has proven to be a selling point in attracting publication buyers, as teachers and parents do not feel they are being taken advantage of by a profit-making book publisher and are willing to pay for the materials. They also like the fact that JUMP Math provides resources to teachers on its website for no cost and that JUMP Math spends less than 10 percent of its budget on administrative expenses, with over 90 percent of its revenues and funds raised going into programs.

While JUMP Math's success at scaling impact cannot be assured, they seem to have a strong likelihood of achieving significant improvement in children's math skills around the world. In my opinion, the key factors working in their favor are their intellectual property, their positive evaluation studies, their limited human-resource needs (and therefore low costs), their alliances with valuable networks, and their earned-income streams. They face challenges from people with different educational philosophies about math education and must continue doing evaluation studies to counter these naysayers and the political and economic entities supporting the old ways of teaching math.

Concluding Comments

Trying to scale a social venture without being ready for it is like trying to run a marathon or triathlon without the right equipment, training, or skills. You will have a much better chance for success—either immediately or at some time in the future—if you are honest with yourself about your readiness to scale the challenges and then take the steps necessary to acquire the appropriate resources and capabilities. Still, unforeseen ecosystem developments can throw even the best prepared social entrepreneur for a loop. In the next chapter, I address how the social entrepreneur can manage his or her fit with the organization's ecosystem to reduce the risks of unanticipated problems and increase the chances of scaling success.

CHAPTER 2

Developing a Scaling Strategy That Fits Your Ecosystem

B
uilding a new house is a complicated process, which can take dozens of skilled workers to complete. I have embarked on projects to build a new home for my family four times, and each experience has been totally unique. All of the projects had highly satisfactory outcomes, but the paths we took to get to those outcomes varied enormously. The way we functioned was highly influenced by the "ecosystem" in which we were operating at the time we began the projects. The whole process was affected by economic, social, and political conditions in the local markets, the changing status of our own economic resources, the shifting tastes and needs of our family members, and the differing philosophies and skills of the various architects, designers, decorators, landscapers, gardeners, bankers, builders, contractors, and subcontractors who teamed up with us. One house was built from a stock plan, another was a brainstorm of a young, aspiring architect who specified everything beforehand, and another was created as we went along, adapting it to our own whims and those of the builder/designer, who would constantly come up with new

ideas for features and materials as he browsed the Internet or searched the overstocked supplies of lumberyards and junk-yards. Clearly, there is no single "right" way to build a house. But the house will come out much better if you adapt to and capitalize on developments in your evolving "ecosystem."

Scaling a social venture can be pursued in many different ways, and there is no perfect, "right" way to do it. However, there are scaling strategies and tactics that have a better "fit" with the ecosystem that a venture faces, and, more often than not, scaling that is more rapid and has a greater impact can be orchestrated when the fit is good. If your ecosystem provides certain resources and opportunities at the start of your scaling efforts, you will want to build on those resources and capital-ize on those opportunities. If your ecosystem contains certain threats to your scaling efforts or has certain resource limitations, you need to develop ways to thwart and overcome those threats and shortcomings. And if your ecosystem is constantly chang-ing or can potentially be changed, through proactive moves on your part to favor scaling even more, then those moves should be entertained. The good builder will take into account all these ecosystem factors in making decisions about land design, mate-rials, HVAC systems, scheduling, and financing, and he will tailor the building program to those factors. If the site has lots of sun or is very sloped, it may make sense to build differently (e.g., passive solar) than if the lot is flat and covered with trees. Likewise, the social entrepreneur has to tailor his scaling efforts to his situational contingencies. If he has lots of volunteers clam-oring to support him and lots of seed funding, then it may make sense to focus on his communications and replication programs rather than on hiring paid staff or fund-raising.

The fundamental idea here is first to learn all you can about the *resource providers, forces and trends,* and *allies and rivals* in your ecosystem. The diagram in Figure 2.1 can be used as a template to guide this examination. Once you have a good

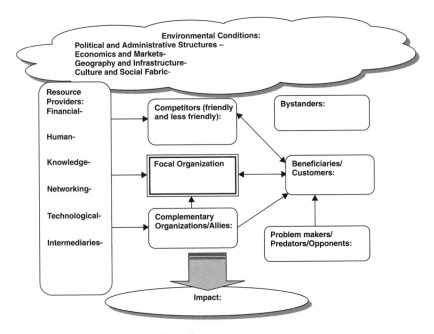

Figure 2.1 An Ecosystem Template

understanding of these facets of your ecosystem, then you should have a clearer notion of which organizational capabilities, or SCALERS, are most crucial to enhance in order to scale successfully. Essentially, when your assessment of your ecosystem tells you that certain starting resources are weak, then building up your organizational capabilities to acquire those resources becomes paramount. On the other hand, when certain starting resources are strong, then you can pay attention to building capabilities to acquire other, less available resources. This inverse relationship between starting resources and needed capabilities will be further influenced by the theory of change you are trying to pursue. If your theory of change is especially dependent on a certain resource, such as labor or money, then the importance of building corresponding capabilities could be made even more essential. The manner in which theories of change, starting resources, and organizational capabilities can interact and affect one another

Figure 2.2   Tasks for Formulating a Scaling Strategy

to produce scaling results is explained in this chapter. The flow diagram in Figure 2.2 shows the tasks to be completed in formulating a sound scaling strategy.

Assessing Resource Providers

It is important to understand where your organization stands with respect to its possession of *human, social, political, financial, technological,* and *natural-resource* capital, as well as its *access to markets.* As discussed in the last chapter, extreme weakness in these areas may suggest that scaling is not right for your organization. Milder weakness in these areas will suggest that you will need to emphasize building certain capabilities over others. Thus, being weak on human capital will mean that the organization needs to focus on the staffing SCALER and recruit, select, train, and supervise the talent needed to lead and manage the organization, serve on boards, motivate and direct volunteers, and provide needed services. Strength in human capital, however, could give the organization the luxury of focusing on other capabilities.

Similarly, weakness in social capital would call for emphasis on communicating and alliance-building, so that more people are persuaded that your services and theory of change are worthy of patronage and support. Strength in this area, in contrast, provides an opportunity for you to make more progress building other capabilities besides communicating and alliance-building.

Weakness in political capital would call for an emphasis on lobbying, but only if some type of government action would tend to benefit your organization, by providing funding, new laws, or law enforcement that could assist you in fulfilling your mission.

Being weak on financial capital would mean that the organization needs to focus on earnings-generation to obtain the funds needed to build other capabilities. Strength in financial capital, in contrast, could allow the organization to make more progress in building capabilities like staffing, communicating, alliance-building, lobbying, and replicating.

A deficit in technological capital, which might manifest itself in the form of weak information systems or inefficient service delivery, would mean that more attention must be paid to developing a replication system that is productive and reliable. Strength in technology at the start might make replication simpler and less challenging.

In some situations, an organization may have limited supplies of the natural resources needed to implement its theory of change. Shortages of agricultural goods, water, fuels, minerals, and so forth can make life difficult for an organization, preventing it from participating in market transactions that could spin off earned income or supply beneficiaries, whereas ample supplies of these natural resources can make it more feasible to participate in certain markets, limiting the need to work on building the capability of stimulating market forces.

Finally, there may be situations in which an organization does not have access to the markets in which it would like to operate because of government restrictions, licensure requirements, collusive behavior, or monopolistic practices. For example, it may not be possible to obtain shelf space for "ethically sourced" products in the most desirable supermarkets. You may need to build the capability of stimulating market forces in order to overcome these entry barriers.

Assessing Forces and Trends

Monitoring and forecasting forces and trends in the external environment of the organization is extremely important, as one's resource situation can be affected by the state of the local and world economies, shifts in political power, migration of populations, global climate change, and even shifts in popular culture (e.g., the rise of Facebook). The best-conceived scaling strategies could be sidetracked by an economic downturn or a drought. Trying to anticipate where these threats might occur—and planning how they can be thwarted to allow scaling to continue—should be a worthwhile exercise.

An example of an organization that was sensitive to external forces and trends is Playworks. Jill Vialet, its founder, monitored trends in education carefully and recognized opportunity in what could be viewed as a disturbing trend. She noted that cost-cutting was eliminating supervised recess and physical education in many low-income elementary schools. She developed a program that now has well-trained instructors leading supervised play experiences during recess at over 300 schools in 22 cities and 18 states, and she is expanding rapidly, with a goal of serving 715 schools by 2015. Schools can actually save money (and trouble) by taking advantage of this program, so Vialet's venture is financed partly by school systems, with the rest coming from grants and donations.[1]

Assessing Allies and Rivals

In approaching the challenge of scaling, it is important to recognize that other organizations are out there that could impact your ability to scale. One needs to consider existing alliances and partnerships and what it would take to make them more productive. What is more, other bystander organizations should be also assessed. What are the pros and cons of forming more formal alliances with them? Can they help add human, social, political, financial, technological, or natural-resource capital to the scaling effort? Indeed, if there are other organizations poised to join forces with you, then that may indicate that you have strength in social capital.

Additionally, you must consider the organizations that compete with you in providing services to beneficiaries. In promoting their organizations, they may be hurting your human, social, political, financial, and natural-resource capital—and they may be providing competition for access to markets. Can you collaborate with these competitors to jointly try to make the overall "pie" bigger, rather than fighting with them for small pieces of the pie? Recently, two leading organizations that provide surgery for children with cleft lips and other facial deformities in the developing world announced plans to merge, ending years in which the groups feuded and competed for donations. The boards of Operation Smile, in Norfolk, Virginia, and Smile Train, in New York, approved the union, which grew quickly out of talks started by the organizations' leaders. "We can reach more children working together than working separately," said Howard Unger, chief operating officer of the older and larger Operation Smile, who will retain his title and manage day-to-day operations for the new group, Operation Smile Train.[2]

Finally, how can you approach organizations that staunchly oppose what you are trying to do? Can you improve your communicating so that your positive messages about your organization overpower any negative messages coming from your opponents? The case can be made that the excellent communications emanating from Teach for America about the contributions it is making to long-term educational reform have overpowered the negative comments about the organization from some representatives of teachers unions, who have complained (not necessarily accurately) about Teach for America recruits taking the jobs of experienced teachers.

Estimating How SCALERS Affect
the Scale of Social Impact

Once you have done a careful assessment of your resource providers, forces and trends, and your allies and rivals, you can give consideration to how well the model presented in Figure 2.3 portrays how scaling might work for your organization. The model proposes that the scale of social impact that an organization achieves will be a function of the effectiveness with which it develops capabilities in the seven SCALERS areas. All other things being equal, the better the organization becomes at staffing, communicating, and so on, the greater social impact it should have—that is, each SCALERS capability should be positively related to the scale of social impact the organization achieves.

The model also proposes that the strength of the relationships between the SCALERS and the scale of social impact achieved will be influenced or moderated by the levels of the starting resources of the organization. Where starting resources are weak, improving the corresponding SCALER capability will have a greater relative effect on scaling success, as compared to where starting resources are strong, when improving the corresponding SCALER capability will not have as large a relative effect on scaling success, in part because "ceiling effects" will limit how much more can be accomplished.

This inverse relationship between starting resources and organizational capabilities is depicted in Figure 2.3 by the negative signs next to the arrows emanating from the different starting resources, indicating that higher levels of the starting resources reduce the strengths of the relationships between capabilities and impact (and vice versa). So, for instance, when human capital is strong at the start, improving your staffing capability should improve your scaling success, but not dramatically. Following similar logic, when financial capital is

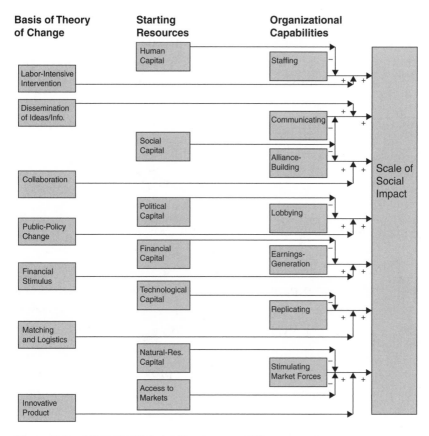

Figure 2.3 SCALERS Model Contingency Effects

weak at the start, improving your earnings-generation capability should improve your scaling success substantially. Thus, the importance of each SCALERS capability in driving scaling success for an organization—and consequently the degree to which the building of different capabilities needs to be emphasized—depends on the resource situation faced at the time the scaling effort is starting.

Figure 2.3 also indicates what the effects of having different types of theories of change will be on the strength of the relationships between the SCALERS and the scale of social impact achieved. An assumption is made that an organization would not pursue a theory of change unless there were pretty good evidence that the theory had validity and that the intervention or program, if executed properly, would have the desired social impacts. Given this assumption, Figure 2.3 therefore suggests that the more your theory of change relies on the provision of labor-intensive services, the stronger the effect will be of improving your staffing capability on your social impact. Similarly, the more your theory of change relies on collaboration, the stronger the effect will be of improving your alliance-building capability on your social impact. Emphasizing other theories of change will have corresponding implications for the effects of other SCALERS capabilities.

Hence, in addition to starting resources, the theory of change pursued by an organization can influence or moderate the importance of each SCALERS capability in driving scaling success. Put more simply, if an organization wants to attack a problem using a certain approach, it had better be good at building the capabilities to implement that approach. Consequently, a theory built around public policy change makes it more important to have lobbying capabilities, while a theory built around selling an innovative product makes it more important to have capabilities at stimulating market forces.

Note that Figure 2.3 represents an oversimplification of the relationships among scaling success, organizational capabilities, starting resources, and theories of change. Many more arrows could have been shown, since it is likely that for most organizations the different SCALERS affect each other and interact with or moderate one another's effects—and potentially other interactions with the starting resources and theories of change exist. Moreover, the diagram does not depict how environmental forces or trends might affect the relationships. Nevertheless, the relationships depicted are a starting point for conducting a deep analysis of what has the potential to drive scaling success in your organization, helping you to find a scaling strategy that will fit well with your ecosystem.

Formulating a Scaling Strategy

Assessing your ecosystem, and considering which organizational capabilities are likely to be most strongly related to scaling success given your resource situation and theory of change, should point you in the direction of a strategy for scaling. You should first attempt to identify a strategy based on the assumption that your ecosystem will remain basically the same. If very little change will occur with your resource providers, forces and trends, and allies and rivals, what will that mean in terms of the relative emphasis you should give to improving your staffing, communicating, alliance-building, lobbying, earnings-generation, replicating, and stimulating market forces? All of these capabilities are likely to deserve some attention for most organizations, but a capability like staffing will require special attention if your theory of change is built around a labor-intensive intervention, your starting human capital is shaky, labor markets are getting tighter, and the allies with whom you might work are unlikely to bring additional human resources to a partnership. At the same time, a capability like lobbying may not require attention if your theory of change does not involve changing public policy and you don't see any threatening policy changes on the horizon.

In a sense, one can envision the challenge of determining a strategy as similar to the challenge faced by the person operating the soundboard during a musical concert. At the concert venue, a group of sliding levers has to be set in different positions, some high, some low, in order to get the sound to mix appropriately for the ears of the audience. For the social entrepreneur, the "levers" of each of the seven SCALERS will have to be set in appropriate positions to reflect the scaling strategy being pursued, with different strategies deploying different mixes of how the variables should be set relative to one another.

Basic Strategic Options: Branching, Affiliation, or Dissemination

There are three traditional pathways to scale, or scaling strategy options: *branching, affiliation, and dissemination*.[3] *Branching* involves growing your own organization to serve more people and places. When an organization like Girls on the Run, which has an after-school self-esteem-enhancement program involving running for girls ages eight to twelve, grows by setting up of 173 councils all over the country that serve 70,000 girls per year, it is essentially branching.[4]

Affiliation involves forming alliances and partnerships to rely on others to implement your theory of change or approach. For example, Computers for Youth (CFY), a New York program that refurbishes discarded computers and distributes them to poor children along with support to enhance their in-home learning environment, has affiliated with several other independent organizations around the country that are involved with similar missions. CFY's Affiliate Network is a diverse, national coalition of independent nonprofit organizations united by a common commitment to improve the home learning environment of low-income families. Network members share best practices, build valuable relationships, and take advantage of discounted products and services to improve the impact of their respective programs. A key objective of the Network is to shape public policy and spread the word about the importance of expanding educational priorities to include learning in the home and the school-home connection. The Affiliate Network currently has 32 members in 22 states and the District of Columbia, and will be expanding to include all 50 states. To help sustain the network, all affiliates pay an annual membership fee and modest fees for specified products and services.[5]

Dissemination involves trying to spread an idea to others through communications and education. For example, City Year seeks to build a citizen-service movement that is larger than its 20-city organization. They promote the idea of community service, encouraging young people to pursue not only the City Year one-year, full-time positions in the cities where it operates, but also to participate in AmeriCorps and Peace Corps programs all over the world.[6]

Using the soundboard analogy, a strategy of branching would probably mean setting the staffing and replicating levers at higher levels than the others. On the other hand, an affiliation strategy would mean putting the alliance-building lever higher, while a dissemination strategy would involve putting the communicating lever higher. But clearly, other mixes of the levers could be possible that are not as easily labeled or as "pure" as branching, affiliation, or dissemination. Indeed, the three organizations cited in the previous paragraph are not pursuing absolutely "pure" strategies, and many organizations have employed all three approaches simultaneously. For instance, the Aravind Eye Hospital in India, known for its delivery of high-quality, low-cost cataract surgeries, has set up branches in several Indian cities, has formed formal partnerships with other hospital systems, and has provided medical education and training to health professionals who are doing cataract surgeries in nonaffiliated institutions.[7]

Adapting Strategy to Shifts in the Ecosystem

Regardless of how you label or visualize your original scaling strategy, you must be prepared to rethink it if your ecosystem undergoes a significant change. Indeed, some organizations will try to effect change in their ecosystems themselves, hoping that this will facilitate the deployment of different scaling strategies that can achieve more in the new environment. An ecosystem can be altered through advocating for new government policies or budget allocations, through persuading bystanders or opponents to become allies or supporters, and through interacting with community leaders to gain acceptance of ideas that could change cultural habits and norms. The last approach has been employed by the African nongovernmental organization Tostan, which has worked for many years to foster sustainable economic development in countries like Senegal, Guinea, Burkina Faso, The Gambia, and Somalia. Tostan has developed a three-year, nonformal education program for adults and adolescents that stresses human rights and strives for community development while honoring the community culture and knowledge systems. The interactions and discussions encouraged by this program have led to a shift in community social norms, which in turn led to numerous communities declaring that they no longer found female genital cutting or child marriage to be acceptable practices. The cessation of these practices, which was not originally a goal of Tostan, has changed the ecosystem and allowed much faster progress to be made in achieving economic empowerment and development, with women playing major roles, in many communities. The new ecosystem allows Tostan's communicating and replicating to be more effective.[8]

Whether your ecosystem changes through your own efforts or through the influence of powerful external forces and trends, a failure to fit well with the ecosystem's changing nature is a recipe for failure at scaling. Road Crew was a social entrepreneurial venture that started with great promise in rural Wisconsin in 2000, but it is no longer around today.

The program's goal was to keep drunk drivers off the road, and it involved having a dispatcher send out car services to people's homes to escort them to and from bars and taverns, keeping them from driving while intoxicated. Indeed, a rigorous evaluation conducted in 2006 found that the program provided thousands of rides and significantly reduced drunk-driving accidents, at a cost of $15,300 per crash avoided—as compared to an average cost per crash of $56,000.

Road Crew was at first supported by nominal fees of $15–$20 that it charged to the passengers, as well as donations from restaurants and bars and government grants, enabling it to expand to 32 communities within a few years. But the program ran into a changing environment and was unable to adapt. Government budgets in Wisconsin, as in many states, were becoming leaner, and officials did not give a program like this as high a priority as other transportation-related programs. Among the reasons for placing a lower priority on this organization was a reasonably widespread attitude among public health advocates that Road Crew was encouraging dangerous levels of binge drinking in rural Wisconsin. The group could not overcome this sentiment through communicating or lobbying and, hence, government grants were then cut, and the business model for Road Crew was no longer viable. Attempts to get the brewing industry to make up the shortfall were unsuccessful, as the industry did not want to be perceived as doing too much to encourage heavy drinking. Charging higher fees for the rides was also not feasible, since it would only lead more drinkers to choose to drive to the drinking establishments instead of using Road Crew. Although clever branding and advertising, along with a rigorous evaluation study, were able to get this venture launched and growing, it ultimately did not fit its evolving ecosystem very well and could not survive.[9]

The Right Fit with the Ecosystem: Girls on the Run

An example of an organization that did a better job of matching its ecosystem is Girls on the Run, which I mentioned earlier in this chapter. This self-esteem-enhancement program for girls eight to thirteen years old teaches them about healthy living and self-respect through activities involving running. It started in Charlotte, North Carolina, in 1996, with a twelve-week, twice-per-week, after-school program for thirteen girls. By 2011, the program had grown to serve 70,000 girls per year through 173 "councils" or franchisees. There are many factors responsible for the scaling success of this program, including the leadership and charisma of the program's founder, Molly Barker, who has been able to inspire others to lead their own councils that often manage programs at multiple sites (e.g., schools, YMCAs, Boys and Girls Clubs). However, the ability of Barker and her management team to fit with several facets of their evolving ecosystem was especially important.

Adapting to the evolving ecosystem is not something that Barker set out to do in a conscious or purposeful way. She saw a variety of individual opportunities for her ideas and initiatives, pursued them aggressively, and these independent actions all came together in a way that clicked and built a national operation with a broad impact. Indeed, the most recent evaluation of the program, reported in a peer-reviewed academic journal, found that the program was definitely increasing the physical activity of the participants, as well as their comfort level with their bodies.[10]

Without labeling them as "resource providers," Barker recognized early on that her program had captured the imagination of the girls and their parents, stimulating word-of-mouth advertising that could generate a steady source of revenue, as parents would gladly pay tuition for an after-school activity that their daughters enjoyed so thoroughly. She also recognized that the enthusiasm for the program was so high that other important resources—coaches and directors of programs that she couldn't produce herself—were willing to work for free as volunteers (the coaches and many of the directors) or as low-paid employees (directors and staff in the larger cities) because they were so committed to the organization's mission. Still other resources that did not require an overwhelming amount of effort came forward in a steady stream, such as sites to hold the program (e.g., schools, YMCAs, Boys and Girls Clubs), sponsors to help with tuition scholarships and shoes for less-advantaged girls (e.g., New Balance), and researchers to do evaluations, which in turn helped with attracting grant funding and sponsorships.

Barker and Girls on the Run also rode the crest of several forces and trends that came to the fore as they were trying to scale. Of particular note was how they were able to capitalize on the huge running boom among women of child-bearing age that took place in the first part of the twenty-first century. In marathons and half-marathons all over the United States, more than half the participants were women. Many of these women wanted to see their daughters obtain the same joy from running that they had obtained, and Girls on the Run provided a way to start them in running. One of the goals of the program was to have the girls complete a 5K run at the end of 12 weeks. The program also tapped into growing parental concerns about childhood obesity and about the phenomenon of "mean girls," both of which the program helps girls cope with. At the same time, the program has steered clear of growing political "hot-button" issues like gay rights and sex education, avoiding being labeled as a "conservative" or "liberal" organization so as not to drive away 50 percent of potential participants.

Another aspect of the ecosystem that served Girls on the Run well was an absence of any organizations that provided serious competition or rivalry for the affection of the girls and their parents, which also helped in attracting support from institutions and sponsors. The only major after-school program in the United States that was focused on serving preteen girls was the Girl Scouts of America, and the characteristics of this program were less oriented toward physical activity and healthy living.

Given Girls on the Run's theory of change that anticipated improving the lives of preteen girls through enrolling them in a program with a well-tested and readily implemented curriculum, and given the ecosystem they faced and the resources available to them, a strategy that enabled rapid scaling was not hard to figure out. While the organization had to pay attention to communicating, alliance-building, and earnings-generation, the two capabilities that seemed to matter most for scaling were staffing and replicating. They needed to keep the flow of volunteer coaches and directors coming, and they needed to have the program copied in neighborhood after neighborhood. It was decided that the best way to make these things happen was to set up what is essentially a franchise system. Each local "council" of Girls on the Run was set up to be an independent 501(c)3, with its own leadership, board of directors, and financial system. Such an arrangement seems to allow a grass-roots enthusiasm to develop around each council, helping to create an esprit de corps that attracts volunteers and supports fund-raising. The latter needs to be done in order to cover administrative expenses for the councils, as well as to offer scholarships to needy girls. Each council does recruitment and fund-raising in its own way—although there is much sharing of best practices across councils to provide guidance—and it is doubtful that a more centrally controlled effort would be as effective as this more grass-roots effort.[11]

A franchise system is not foolproof and, especially if the national or local ecosystems shift, there may be some franchises that do better than others. There have been several Girls on the Run councils that have been abandoned. The local council of Girls on the Run in my area, Girls on the Run of the Triangle, certainly faced challenges during the recent recession and even had to cut scholarships and let personnel go. But they adapted to the shifting ecosystem by making major changes in their fund-raising approaches while remaining steadfast in their commitment to serving more girls of more different ethnic backgrounds in more communities in the Raleigh-Durham, North Carolina, area.

The new fund-raising and expansion approaches fed off each other. Having more girls from more areas enrolled in the program attracted more people to fund-raising events and led to more funds being generated. So instead of having a springtime 5K race in smallish Chapel Hill serve as the council's major fund-raising event, they shifted the spring race to a larger venue in downtown Durham and drew many more participants. They also persuaded other local running races and triathlons to make Girls on the Run a financial beneficiary, offering to bring the girls from the program to serve at water stations and as finish-line supporters. Furthermore, they changed from having a "girls night out" at the local Nordstrom's department store, which only brought in funds through ticket sales (to get admission to the store and a little bit of wine and snacks on a Sunday evening), to having a "family night" at Southern Season, a magnificent gourmet food store. This new event drew many more people and generated funds from admission tickets, from a percentage of everything people bought that evening (and people bought a lot!), and from a $100-a-plate VIP dinner at the store's fine restaurant, during which the Duke University's women's basketball coach gave a rousing speech. The financial picture of this council has turned completely around, and many more girls are benefiting from its programs.

Concluding Comments

Building and growing a venture that doesn't fit its ecosystem is like trying to build a golf course in the mountains of Alaska. There are better design concepts with better conservation properties more suited to the Alaskan climate. The social entrepreneurial organization should obtain a deep understanding of its ecosystem and design a scaling strategy that fits the ecosystem well. Through examining its resource providers, forces and trends, and allies and rivals—and then assessing how they all work together to potentially affect how the different organizational capabilities (i.e., SCALERS) are related to scaling success—the organization can determine a strategy that articulates how much emphasis it wants to give to each of the seven SCALERS. This strategy should not be set in stone and should be adaptable or capable of being changed in response to changes in the ecosystem caused by either external forces or the scaling actions of the organization itself. Thoughts about what those scaling actions might be like in each of the seven capability categories are presented in the next seven chapters.

CHAPTER 3

Staffing: Building Your Human Resources Capability

The Skoll World Forum on Social Entrepreneurship has been held every spring since 2004 in stately Oxford, England. The Forum is co-produced by the Skoll Foundation, which was founded by Jeff Skoll, the first President of eBay, and the Skoll Centre at the University of Oxford which was founded with an initial investment from this philanthropist. The Forum is used, in part, to announce the annual Skoll Foundation Award Winners—a group of accomplished social entrepreneurs who have been chosen to receive new, multiyear funding from the foundation. Many of the "big name" social entrepreneurs treat the Forum as a kind of "Academy Awards" event and attend every year, using it as a time to network, fundraise, and learn from one another. I have had the privilege of attending the Forum four times, and each time I have been inspired and in awe of the social entrepreneurs I have met or seen. I am convinced that the social entrepreneurs who have been chosen to attend the Forum as either award winners or speakers are a special breed. They exhibit enormous passion and excitement for what they are doing and possess the kind of magnetism and persuasion abilities that make you want follow them into "battle" as either an employee, a volunteer, or a donor.

Several years ago during this event, I was attending an evening reception in one of Oxford University's historic halls with my son. In this very crowded and noisy environment, we found ourselves standing next to former Skoll awardee Wendy Kopp, the founder of Teach for America, the program that recruits thousands of recent college graduates to teach in inner-city schools for two years. I reintroduced myself to Kopp, reminding her that we had met once before at a Duke University event. Surprisingly, my son didn't know about Teach for America at the time, and he embarrassed me a little by asking Kopp what it was. Her reaction to this question astounded me. Instead of trying to give a quick answer so that she could then move on to speaking to more important people at the reception (like potential funders), she looked my son in the eye, raised her voice to be heard clearly in the noisy hall, and gave a passionate and eloquent two-minute "elevator pitch" about the mission and accomplishments of Teach for America. Here is a woman who had been on the cover of *Fortune* magazine and had won virtually all the honors a social entrepreneur could win, talking to us with a level of excitement about her work that was infectious, not really knowing who we were or what we could do for her.

The passionate and inspiring leadership of people like Kopp can make a huge difference when you are trying to scale a social venture. For that reason, there are funders of social entrepreneurs who place considerable weight on the leadership qualities of the founder when deciding which social ventures to support. For example, Bill Draper, the Silicon Valley venture capitalist who also cofounded the Draper-Richards Foundation that supports social entrepreneurs, has stated this about the importance of leadership:

> We spend extensive time getting to know these social entrepreneurs. Our foundation partners want to understand their vision, as well as their capacity to manage people, strategically assess opportunities, communicate effectively, show grace under pressure, bring monetary and human resources to their organization, and exhibit the highest levels of integrity in all circumstances. We believe these are skills that lead to the growth of extraordinary organizations.[1]

But Draper and others recognize that it takes much more than great leadership to keep a social venture flourishing. A wide range of human resource and staffing capabilities must be cultivated and maintained. Kopp has surrounded herself with many competent managers while Teach for America has grown, and the organization has also refined its approach to recruiting and retaining teachers/volunteers.

In some cases, however, a founder will need to step aside and let more professional managers take over. The founder's passion and excitement can achieve the launch and attract important initial financing, but delivering on deadlines and attaining certain performance benchmarks often takes another set of skills. For example, Room to Read was founded by John Wood, and he has done a great job of building initial enthusiasm for his venture and attracting awards and funding. He has won Skoll and Draper-Richards awards for his programs, which are described on the Room to Read website in the following way:

> Our Reading Room program provides libraries to children so they can read and explore. Our Local Language Publishing program allows children to read books in their mother tongue. Our School Room program gives children a safe place to learn. Our Girls' Education program enables girls to enroll in and stay in

school. We currently work in Bangladesh, Cambodia, India, Laos, Nepal, South Africa, Sri Lanka, Vietnam and Zambia—with plans to expand so we can bring educational opportunities and resources to children throughout the developing world.[2]

However, Wood recognized rather early on that he needed more professional management support to scale Room to Read and have greater impact. He has stated:

> There is this challenge of being an entrepreneur, where you start something up, but ultimately, you don't want to run it. If you haven't successfully turned it over to someone else, then you haven't succeeded as an entrepreneur. And that's why I basically decided that by our ten-year anniversary, I didn't want to be CEO of Room to Read. I wanted to have someone else be CEO, have that person surrounded by a management team, and let myself be the ambassador of Room to Read, as opposed to running things on a day-to-day basis.[3]

Erin Ganju became that chief executive officer, after first joining Room to Read in 2001 as chief operating officer. Prior to that, Ganju had worked as a product line manager at Unilever and as a financial analyst at Goldman Sachs. She was able to put her strong project management skills to use at Room to Read, helping to develop a strategy for entering new countries, formalizing program design, and helping channel Wood's fundraising talents into specific program areas. Ganju enjoyed managing operations, talent, and processes, while Wood preferred public speaking, fundraising, and building a worldwide network of allies.[4]

The staffing organizational capability is defined here as:

> the effectiveness of the organization at filling its labor needs, including its managerial posts and board memberships, with paid staff or volunteers who have the requisite skills for the

needed positions and who are organized and managed in ways that will encourage the achievement of desired social changes.

Being effective at staffing (like Teach for America and Room to Read have been) means having:

- inspiring leadership;
- managers with planning and supervision skills;
- board members who contribute monetarily and/or with know-how;
- productive recruiting and training programs;
- employees or volunteers capable of delivering high-quality services or solutions to problems; and
- roles and responsibilities for employees and volunteers that are understood and function well.

Thus, a range of human resource management capabilities must be developed in order for an organization to be considered effective at staffing, not just having effective leadership or competent professional staff members. The staffing SCALER becomes especially important for achieving success in situations where the organization's theory of change involves the delivery of labor-intensive services or problem solutions. It becomes even more important when the scaling effort commences at a time when the organization's ecosystem is weak on human capital, but has enough financial capital to support the improvement of that human capital. In order to improve competence at staffing, it takes money for recruitment, salaries, and benefits. If money for this is not readily available, it may be best to try to scale by building competences in areas like communicating, alliance-building, lobbying, and replicating (along, of course, with earnings-generation). Building these competences, rather than staffing, may also be important if prosperous economic trends are making it difficult to attract and retain new personnel, who may have more lucrative opportunities in the for-profit sector. Of course, there still needs to be a base of competent people managing things no matter what, or else the whole organization can fall apart.

Building the Staffing Capability

When scaling can only be accomplished by adding to your human resource capabilities, then you need to do hard work to build up your excellence in recruiting, training, organizing, managing, and retaining the people you need to implement your programs and solutions. Sometimes you can reduce this work—or at least the expenses associated with the work—by using volunteers, animals, or machines to deliver services. For example, Girls on the Run uses volunteer coaches to deliver its program to 70,000 girls per year, and many of the managerial posts at its 173 councils are filled by unpaid or low-paid individuals who are passionately committed to the cause of helping the lives of preteen girls. Another organization, which relies on animals to deliver services, is Apopo, which uses giant rats to do land-mine detection and tuberculosis testing in Mozambique and Tanzania. On the other hand, organizations like Kiva or DonorsChoose deliver services using machines, which have software programs that help match donors with needy organizations or individuals (such as teachers). But all these service-delivery mechanisms require recruiting, training, organizing, and managing by competent people. So there are very few social entrepreneurial organizations that can prosper without paying serious attention to their staffing capability. Yet one should not go overboard in emphasizing this capability.

Indeed, I have met numerous people in the social entrepreneurship field, including many donors/funders and consultants, who focus on the human resource capacities of social entrepreneurial organizations more than anything else, often overlooking the importance of other equally significant capabilities.

There seems to be a philosophy developing among some observers that human-resource "capacity-building" is the "secret sauce" that leads to success. All you need to do is find an inspiring leader, surround him or her with talented, committed people who are assigned clear roles and responsibilities, and everything else falls into place. But a study by the W. K. Kellogg Foundation, which is one of the few examples available of an investigation into why a social entrepreneurial venture *failed*, points to the limitations of this thinking. The Foundation's independent evaluator reports that SeaChange, a venture that tried to use technology to match social entrepreneurs with donors and investors, in which the Foundation had invested $735,000 and total fund-raising had come to $2.45 million, "lacked a strong business plan, had hired senior managers before it had anything for them to manage, that its board members and staff could not define a "social entrepreneur," and that the chief executive's charisma had masked shortcomings in his management skills."[5] In my mind, this situation argues that effectiveness at human-resource capacity building is a *necessary* condition for success, but it is not a *sufficient* condition for this success. A strong business plan, which should include attention to all the other organizational capabilities, is ultimately the key determinant of success.

Recruiting

To avoid the fate of a SeaChange, which ended up being merged into another nonprofit, an organization clearly cannot ignore human resource capacity building. But neither can it rely solely on its actions in that area to be all it needs to do in order to scale. Creating this capability first involves being effective at recruiting talent. One of the best in this department is Teach for America, which has figured out how to make accomplished college graduates flock to its two-year program of teaching in inner-city schools for modest pay. Teach for America has analyzed past data to figure out at which college campuses it is most likely to recruit top graduates. For example, they know that 12 percent of all graduates of Ivy League schools applied to Teach for America in 2010. On those campuses where they recruit, they have disseminated persuasive messages about the value of joining Teach for America for achieving career aspirations, creating a buzz or word-of-mouth about the opportunity that has made receiving an offer from Teach for America seem like the winning of a Nobel Prize.[6] Teach for America's recruiting skill has undoubtedly been a key driver in its ability to scale social impact.

It is one thing to recruit young people into short-term, low-paying jobs that at least provide marketable credentials, and quite another to recruit experienced managers to longer-term, modest-paying jobs that have difficult challenges, frequently in the area of fund-raising. Moreover, recruiting board members with financial resources and skills is another important but difficult task for most organizations. I have been the member of two different boards of social purpose organizations, and both have had to deal with several changeovers of executive directors and board members. One organization treated the recruiting of new executive directors and board members in a very systematic fashion, setting up search committees with well-defined procedures and using an outside (pro-bono) consultant to help screen candidates. Concerted efforts to "spread the word" about the opportunities were mounted, using carefully placed advertising but also encouraging word-of-mouth referrals. The other organization recruited in a much less systematic fashion, with the organization's founder totally controlling both types of searches. The executive-director candidates mostly came from responses to advertising, not from word-of-mouth referrals, and the new board members were all friends of the founder. Although numerous other factors have certainly affected the fortunes of these organizations, the one that has done more systematic recruiting has been able to scale more dramatically and keep talent longer than the other one, which has remained mired in a precarious financial state and has not really grown, even though it provides a very valuable and desired public service.

The benefits of being analytic and systematic about recruiting should also pay dividends in trying to attract volunteers. In particular, research should be done to determine the motives that people have for volunteering for your organization. Are they volunteering because they believe so deeply in your cause and want to help in any way that they can, seeing the donation of time as more feasible for them than money? Volunteers to Girls on the Run may be motivated in this way, as could the volunteers to organizations like Challah for Hunger, which gets students on college campuses to bake and deliver holiday bread loaves in their communities in order to obtain revenue for supporting hunger and disaster relief.[7] But other motives for volunteering can also come into play, such as a desire for a bonding social experience (e.g., building a house together for Habitat for Humanity) or a need to show meaningful work experience on one's résumé (e.g., creating a website for a social venture). Another motive could be earning respect in one's community, which may partially explain why 62,000 people volunteer to teach in the Pratham elementary schools in India, even though their chances of using this voluntary teaching experience as a stepping-stone to paying teaching jobs are probably very slim.[8] Whether you are recruiting volunteers, employees, managers, or board members, you should be able to create more effective appeals and messages if you have a good grasp of the motives people have for engaging with your organization.

Training

Helping your employees, managers, board members, and volunteers acquire the skills they need for their positions can be a very important element in scaling success. For example, training health care workers in narrower, specialized skills has been crucial to organizations like Aravind Eye Hospitals (which does cataract surgeries in India) and Partners in Health (which combats infectious diseases in Haiti and other parts of the developing world). They could have never grown if they were limited to recruiting nurses and physician's assistants with more general skills, but who are more expensive and have been trained by others.

Proper training can make a major difference in whether the quality of programs meets or exceeds the expectations of those who are being served. Teachers need to be trained in how to use innovative curricular materials, and substance abuse counselors need to be trained in how to introduce new therapies and treatments. Lack of appropriate training can undermine the quality of interventions, making it impossible for successes to build on successes. And training can be important even when more sophisticated services are not being provided as part of the organization's theory of change. Training people in how to do administrative tasks more efficiently or in how to deal with customer inquiries and complaints can pay dividends through improving efficiency and creating goodwill.

Organizing and Managing

Besides being able to recruit talented people successfully, you should also be able to organize and manage those people, so that they can operate in an efficient and effective manner in implementing your theory of change. The fields of management and organizational behavior are filled with prescriptions on how to manage and lead organizations under various conditions, and it would take pages and pages to summarize the lessons that can be drawn from this work. What is clear from all this analysis, however, is that there is no one right way to lead and organize people, and the best approach will depend on an enormous number of factors both internal and external to the organization. Moreover, one must be prepared to engage in a little bit of trial and error to get leadership and organizing right for the given situation.

Retaining People

Avoiding a constant turnover of talented people has been a challenge for most social purpose organizations. Frankly, the compensation tends to be lower in these organizations, and people frequently find that the psychic rewards of working in this sector—or of being part of an exciting "team" that is having social impact—cannot, as financial demands pile up, compensate for the income sacrifice. Well-designed performance appraisal systems that rely on positive feedback more than negative feedback can help to keep the psychic rewards working in your favor, but this may not be enough.

It is terribly important to let your most talented people see their positions as stepping-stones to personal development and career advancement. If they view their jobs as "dead ends" or as increasingly boring, then they will seek other opportunities as soon as possible. But if you help them see that strong job performance will create a path to more challenging, interesting, and responsible positions within your organization—and that this in turn can lead to better financial compensation within your organization or lucrative offers from other organizations—you may be able to keep them working harder for you and for a few years longer. You will typically be better off retaining great people for shorter periods of time than keeping mediocre people until they retire.

Putting a Winning Team Together: Playworks

Supervising school recess periods is not for everyone, even if one has a guidebook or well-tested program to follow that seems to keep the kids happy, healthy, and nonconfrontational. There are people who really take to this task, see it as exciting and challenging, and have a gift for getting children to follow them like the Pied Piper. At the same time, there are others who are easily frustrated by the chaos of recess and should be seeking other ways to help children.

Playworks, the program introduced earlier that manages recess for over 170,000 children in over 300 schools in 22 cities, has recognized that finding the right people to be their recess "coaches" is crucial to its ability to have an impact, so the recruiting, training, managing, and retaining of these people is controlled carefully by the home office in Oakland, California. Ineffective coaches can not only destroy a Playworks program at a single school, but also create bad word-of-mouth that can poison opportunities at other schools or in an entire school system. In budget-stretched schools around the United States, the purchase of the Playworks program is a "big ticket" item that costs each school in the neighborhood of $25,000 per year. Relationships with principals and administrators have to be cultivated, nurtured, and enhanced, and the *control* of this through a branching approach makes much more sense than trying to do it with franchising, which is the approach employed by Girls on the Run (discussed in the last chapter).

The determinant for whether to have branching (like Playworks) versus franchising (like Girls on the Run) has a lot to do with the tasks needed on the ground. For example, less is expected of the Girls on the Run coaches than those coaching for Playworks. The former just have to deal with preteen girls who have entered the program willingly (or at least with parental encouragement) and must be advised and encouraged for 12 weeks using a well-tested curriculum. The latter has to deal with more gender and ethnic diversity and be able to deploy a "bag of tricks" on the spur of the moment in a potentially explosive playground setting with positive results. If a coach is weak and a girl leaves the program, it costs the local council of Girls on the Run at most a few hundred dollars. If a coach is weak and a principal drops the Playworks program, which is a rare event, it can cost in the tens of thousands of dollars. Furthermore, it will be much more expensive to replace Playworks coaches than the volunteer Girls on the Run coaches. So the differences in the business models of the two organizations—with Girls on the Run relying heavily on unpaid volunteers and Playworks relying heavily on paid coaches and paying principals—makes franchising better for one and branching better for the other.

Jill Vialet, who founded Playworks in 1996 and still serves as its CEO, recognized that AmeriCorps volunteers would be the best candidates to become coaches, as they have a helping mindset and they also receive a subsidy from the federal government of $12,000–$13,000 per year. She figures that she can put a coach in a school to manage all of its recesses for $55,000 per year, with $25,000 coming from the school budget, $12,000 to $13,000 coming from AmeriCorps, and the rest coming from donations and fund-raising. The first-year coaches are paid $26,000 per year, and they receive health benefits. Additional revenue is generated for Playworks by providing schools with after-school leadership-development and sports programs for the children and by doing other forms of professional-development training for teachers and support staff.

By expanding primarily into cities that have ample supplies of AmeriCorps volunteers, Vialet ensured herself of having a steady pipeline of coaching candidates. More than half of their schools have AmeriCorps coaches, and the others seem to be able to identify coaching candidates more easily. Nevertheless, the skills and empathetic nature that make someone an effective recess coach cannot be identified simply by looking at resumés and conducting face-to-face interviews, although this still must be done to narrow the pool of candidates. Vialet discovered that the best way to select coaches was by watching candidates lead games with other potential coaches and staff members. She has developed a series of games that she uses for this purpose, as well as to help her select the executive directors for the local branches and other staffers. She has also made use of headhunters and employment counselors to identify executive director candidates. The recently hired executive director of the new Durham, North Carolina, branch of Playworks was identified by an outside firm.

Once hired, coaches and staffers go through two weeks (80 hours) of preservice training that teaches them how to manage recess effectively. They learn how to introduce games and activities and determine teams without embarrassing anyone, and they practice how to resolve conflicts (mostly with a rock-paper-scissors shoot-out) and deal with disobedience and bullying. Other training takes place for entire days during the year and during a week-long summer camp, and considerable networking and knowledge-sharing occurs at these sessions. The training is carried out by experienced coaches who have seen it all, giving them credibility and influence over the new recruits.

In fact, the whole organization is populated all the way up to the top by former coaches and staff members, leading the new recruits to see Playworks as having career advancement opportunities, not as just a place to try something different while in AmeriCorps. For example, Elizabeth Cushing, named president and chief operating officer in October of 2011, started with the organization in 2004 as director of evaluation, moving on from that to director of development and chief strategy officer before advancing to the new position. Employees are paid a fair wage (for a nonprofit) commensurate with their responsibilities, and health insurance is provided. All of these factors have kept turnover manageable and created a fun and supportive working atmosphere. Seventy percent of the coaches stay for at least two years.

As the organization has grown, Vialet has recognized that she cannot have her hands in everything and has delegated more and more work to professional staff. She focuses on being the external voice of the organization, on fund-raising, and on generating innovations. She believes in "adaptive leadership" and floating new and wild ideas to see if they catch on. She leaves a lot of the day-to-day work to others, such as expansion planning, financial management, recruiting, and marketing, and she has hired some "outsiders" who possess skills in these areas to fill these roles. With more than 300 schools to serve and more than 450 employees, delegation is essential.[9] Regardless, the team seems to be functioning extremely well, and recent evaluation data indicates that

- nearly nine out of ten schools (88%) reported a decrease in the number of conflicts originating on the playground and spilling over into the classroom;
- 85% reported a reduction in the amount of time transitioning from recess to classroom instruction;

- nationally, Playworks schools averaged *more than 24 hours of reclaimed teaching time* from resolving playground issues;
- in addition, 86% reported a decrease in incidents of bullying, and 87% reported a decrease in disciplinary referrals.[10]

Playworks' rapid expansion seems poised to continue.

Concluding Comments

A social venture cannot scale successfully without talented people. You must have charismatic, inspiring, and persuasive leadership, while also being effective at recruiting, training, organizing, managing, and retaining the human resources you need to implement your theory of change and scale your impact. But effective staffing is a necessary condition for scaling success, not a sufficient one. It can be shortsighted to overemphasize the accumulation of talent, thinking that the "secret sauce" to success is simply having great leadership along with enthusiastic, skilled employees and volunteers. Even incredibly gifted leaders like Wendy Kopp of Teach for America or John Wood of Room to Read, and all the terrific people who work with them, could not have had the impacts they have had without being extremely effective at building the other six SCALERS capabilities. Yes, many of these capabilities can be improved by having superior talent—and others, like communicating and earnings-generation, can help you attract superior talent—but staffing will typically only be one of several important ingredients in the recipe for scaling success.

CHAPTER 4

Communicating: Achieving Buy-In from Key Stakeholders

"Social marketing," as it has traditionally been viewed, refers to efforts to persuade people to engage in behaviors that benefit both themselves and society. When you persuade people to wear sunscreen religiously, you are protecting them from skin cancer and you are also saving others the expense of having to pay higher insurance premiums or higher taxes to cover the costs that health care providers or governments incur when treating people for skin cancer. Although the term "social marketing" has recently been used to describe marketing efforts that make use of social media like Facebook, I am more comfortable with the old meaning and have spent a good part of my career doing research and teaching on this topic. I have worked on problems like how to persuade people to avoid drinking and driving, cease smoking, eat more fruits and vegetables, limit their use of credit, and get mammograms and other cancer screening tests.

Social marketing can be extremely challenging. You typically are seeking to get people to change entrenched and even addictive behaviors, and you often have other marketing efforts to compete with that are urging them to continue these behaviors. Think of all the marketing that encourages people to eat poorly, drive fast, use tobacco products, and consume alcohol. Social marketers need to counter these types of campaigns while trying to teach, motivate, and facilitate socially beneficial behaviors that people have previously resisted. Social marketing normally seeks to get people to change their behaviors voluntarily, not through coercion. Initiatives that pursue coercive means to change behaviors, such as through threatening fines or jail sentences, are better labeled as forms of lobbying or advocacy.

One of the most difficult social marketing challenges I have studied is how to persuade pregnant women to abstain from drinking alcohol. Mothers who drink put their babies at risk for developing fetal alcohol spectrum disorders (FASD) or, in the most extreme cases, fetal alcohol syndrome. The challenge of getting pregnant women to abstain from alcohol has parallels to the challenges faced by many social purpose organizations in the development of communicating capabilities. Many of these organizations face great difficulty convincing people to change entrenched behaviors, such as engaging in unprotected sex or maxing out credit cards. Organizations that have encountered challenges in communicating to pregnant women about alcohol can provide insight to guide those who face challenges in changing other behaviors.

It has proven very hard to prevent FASD in the United States and all around the world. Women can prevent these disorders through an easy-to-understand behavior: don't drink alcohol when you're pregnant, and warning labels on US alcoholic beverages and recommendations from all US government agencies and medical societies state that pregnant women should abstain from alcohol. Yet pregnant women still drink—surveys suggest that as many as 12 percent of US pregnant women consume at least one drink per week.[1] The consequence of this is that as many as 5 percent of children born in the United States suffer from FASD,[2] although sufferers are often diagnosed with attention deficit hyperactivity disorder (ADHD) instead of FASD. The reasons pregnant women still drink are complicated. Some do so because their doctors are ill-informed and tell them that light drinking is OK. Others simply don't know that drinking is dangerous to their fetuses and have not processed the information on the warning labels. Still others have an addiction or dependence on alcohol that they cannot break.

Clearly, to combat FASD, organizations like the March of Dimes and the National Organization of Fetal Alcohol Syndrome (NOFAS) need to execute much better communications programs. They must both persuade more donors to finance their campaigns, and they have to do better at persuading doctors, pregnant women, and the general public that women who are expecting should abstain from drinking. Developing this capability is probably the most important task these organizations need to execute to achieve their goals of a significant reduction of fetal alcohol spectrum disorders. All the capacity building in the world in terms of staffing and infrastructure will not help them at all if they cannot overcome this communications challenge.

The communicating organizational capability is defined here as:

> the effectiveness with which the organization is able to persuade key stakeholders that its change strategy is worth adopting and/or supporting

The communicating SCALER becomes especially important for achieving success in situations where the organization's theory of change involves disseminating ideas and information. It becomes even more important when the effort commences at a time when the organization's ecosystem is weak on social capital, but has enough financial capital to support the improvement of that social capital. Improving competence at communicating takes money for developing, testing, and distributing messages, and if money for this is not readily available, it may be best to try to scale by building competences in areas like alliance-building, lobbying, and replicating (along with, of course, earnings-generation).

Communications and Elephant Riding

Successful communicating often cannot be accomplished without considerable research and systematic trial and error. This is the particularly the case for communications designed to change the behavior of the beneficiaries of a social venture, but it is also the case for communications aimed at investors, employees, volunteers, and the general public. Among the behavior-change messages that have proven incredibly difficult to communicate are: don't drink when pregnant, don't drink and drive, don't use addictive drugs, don't have unprotected sex, and don't overeat. Many social entrepreneurs have been stopped in their tracks by how difficult it is to achieve behavior changes like these.

Take, for example, Jamie Oliver, the British celebrity chef, and his social entrepreneurial effort to achieve a "Food Revolution," changing the junk-food eating habits of young Americans. In spite of his highly acclaimed reality television program broadcast on the ABC network, in which he was filmed in Huntington, West Virginia, working with school officials, cafeteria workers, restaurants, parents, and children to help them learn how to cook, appreciate, and demand healthier foods (especially fruits and vegetables), his efforts have achieved very little impact on children's eating habits there. An evaluation study done in Huntington showed disappointing results from Jamie's interventions. Moreover, when he tried to follow-up the Huntington filming with another set of interventions in the Los Angeles, California, area, the public schools there rebuffed him, and the new season of the show became the story of how he is seeking change through other avenues.[3]

In thinking about the challenge of getting people to change entrenched behaviors like eating junk food, I have been attracted to a framework developed by my Duke University colleague, Dan Heath, and his brother, Chip Heath, in their best-selling book *Switch*.[4] The authors liken the challenge of persuading people to change their behavior to the challenge of riding an elephant. They argue that to achieve behavioral change one must (1) direct the rider, (2) motivate the elephant, and (3) shape the path.

Directing people what to do is the first task and, in the case of eating too much junk food, the message is simple (Don't!), but its processing on the part of people has been limited. Theories of behavior change, such as social cognitive theory, suggest that knowledge alone is necessary but not sufficient to change behavior. People must be *motivated* to change, be confident they can change, and have the skills to change. Oliver was charming and extremely likable with the Huntington children, but he probably wasn't very motivating to a bunch of young people who think they are going to live forever and hate to deny themselves short-term pleasures like ice cream, sugared soft drinks, and fatty pizza. Making it unbelievably easy and convenient for children to eat healthier—or essentially *shaping the path* for the desired behavior by doing things like offering only healthy options in cafeteria lines or vending machines and making the healthy food much cheaper than the unhealthy food—may accomplish more. Unfortunately, Oliver could only do so much to influence the options and prices available to Huntington children, and he had severe difficulties getting the Los Angeles public schools to work with him at all.

In Australia, public health officials have been able to get many more people to protect themselves from sun exposure by (1) constantly reminding (directing) people of the benefits of preventive actions (with a "Slip! Slop! Slap!" media campaign: slipping on a shirt, slopping on sunscreen, and slapping on a hat), (2) scaring (motivating) them about the danger of skin cancer if they don't take these precautions (with a "SunSmart" campaign), and (3) making it much more convenient (shaping) to take protective actions by making sunscreen available in most localities, having dispensers in many restrooms right beside the soap dispensers, and by also promoting the development and use of sun-protective clothing.

Hospice care has also scaled through effective communications. Health, social-work, and faith advisers have become more assertive in directing patients to hospice organizations, which have improved their ability to motivate patients and their families to avail themselves of palliative care by showing how compassionate and helpful it can be. Moreover, the path to taking advantage of this care has been made easier through the development of numerous at-home hospice operations.

Another example of successful communications to beneficiaries is provided by OPOWER, a small software company that works with public utilities. They have especially succeeded in motivating people to conserve energy by sending statements that report on household consumption—*and* on the average household consumption of their neighbors. People seem to have a strong desire to beat their neighbors once this comparative information is provided. By the end of 2010, despite reaching just a little over a million homes, the amount of energy use reduced by OPOWER was the equivalent to removing 150,000 homes from the electricity grid.[5]

As suggested at the start of this chapter, an example of less successful communications can be found in attempts to persuade pregnant women to abstain from alcohol. Unfortunately, the directions provided to the "rider" have often been ambiguous, as many doctors still tell their pregnant patients that light drinking is not potentially harmful to their babies. A recent survey of members of the American College of Obstetricians and Gynecologists found that only 66 percent of the respondents believed that "occasional alcohol consumption is not safe during any period of pregnancy," which explains why many doctors were not as vigilant about warning their patients as they could have been (although 78 percent said they did recommend abstinence).[6] Unfortunately, while scientific research is increasingly discovering evidence that even small amounts of drinking can harm the fetus, these findings are disseminating slowly.[7]

Additionally, while one would think arousing a woman's motivation to protect her baby would not be difficult at all, it has proven hard to influence pregnant women to give up alcohol totally, since they are being asked to give up so many things while pregnant that they sometimes don't know which scientific reports to trust. Finally, the path for a pregnant woman may not really be suited for abstinence, as turning down a drink in a social situation may not be easy for a woman to do, especially if she does not want others to know she is pregnant.[8] Thus, health communicators need to develop clearer directions, more motivational messages, and more comfortable ways for women to say no to alcohol in social situations.

The Heaths' direct, motivate, and shape framework can also apply when you are communicating to investors, donors, employees, volunteers, and others. In most cases, you want these audiences to change their behavior too, but usually not behaviors that affect their physical health. Investors and donors are often more likely to open their wallets if they are directed to specific options for giving, such as to support an identified needy person or a new innovative program. You can often arouse motivation through stories about the good works of the organization, but motives to look good to others (e.g., friends, customers, regulators) due to one's generosity can sometimes also be aroused. Along these lines, media publicity can often be a spur to donations, since some people like to know that the cause they are supporting is well recognized by others. For example, the organization KIVA, which matches donors and needy organizations in an online format, got a significant uptick in donations after a PBS *Frontline* report aired about it.[9] Finally, the path can be shaped for investors/donors by making giving easy, fun, and discreet, allowing donations to be made online (like KIVA) or as part of social events like galas, auctions, or races.

The importance of connecting to people's motives when trying to recruit and retain employees and volunteers was stressed in the previous chapter. Additionally, directing them very clearly about what to do (e.g., well-defined roles and responsibilities, articulated in carefully crafted job descriptions) and also shaping the path to make it easier for them to apply for positions and to match themselves with volunteer opportunities (e.g., using online applications and matching programs) can help to produce desired responses.

Beyond Elephant Riding

Research on behavior-change communications has produced several other pieces of advice for guiding scaling attempts.[10] One basic discovery is that *tailoring* messages to the tastes, preferences, and abilities of individuals or market segments is more effective than trying to persuade people through using generic messages that are supposed to appeal to everyone. In other words, it is better to go after behavior-change targets (or elephants) with rifles rather than shotguns. Thus, one set of messages should probably be used to persuade pregnant high school-dropout teenage girls not to drink alcohol, while another set of messages should be used to appeal to pregnant, college-educated, middle-aged women. The former set of messages might be more emotional and directive, while the latter set could be more rational and science-based.

Tailoring messages all the way down to the individual level has helped Mothers2Mothers persuade pregnant women with human immunodeficiency virus/acquired immune deficiency syndrome (HIV/AIDS) in sub-Saharan Africa to take drugs to protect their unborn children from getting the disease. Mothers who have successfully protected their own children have in turn been hired and trained to tailor personal appeals to newly pregnant women.[11]

Another finding is that it is more effective to encourage people to *commence a new behavior* than it is to try to get them to cease an old behavior. Hence, people should be encouraged to wear sunscreen instead of being urged not to go out in the sun. Moreover, the research suggests that getting people to take up a new behavior will be more likely if you build the *self-efficacy* of the message recipient. Let people know that the sunscreen works if they are attentive about applying it.

The Importance of Research

Besides persuasive message content, you also need credible spokespersons, efficient media, and regularly refreshed content, as the "wearing-out" or "tuning-out" of a message often occurs. The best spokesperson may not be the most easily recognized celebrity or athlete, as audiences may not see that person as trustworthy. But some well-known spokespersons have done an enormous amount for their causes—just think of what Bono has done for the Global Fund for HIV/AIDS, or what President Jimmy Carter has done for Habitat for Humanity. To see how people react to your spokespersons, or, for that matter, any features of your communications effort, it is worthwhile to conduct copy tests of your messages. This can be done with online surveys with prerecruited samples of people (from organizations like Qualtrics, SurveyMonkey, Zoomerang, and Lightspeed), where some people are randomly assigned to see one message, and another group is randomly assigned to see another message. The messages can then be compared in terms what beliefs, attitudes, and intentions they produce. This is an inexpensive way to obtain valuable guidance for your communications efforts.

Research can also guide your choices of media through your doing surveys of targeted audiences to determine their media habits, and it can also guide decisions about how frequently to send out messages and whether they need to be changed. Doing tracking surveys over time to see how beliefs, attitudes, intentions, and reported behaviors are shifting can help with this, and it can also help you document the kind of return on investment you are getting from your communications.

Keep Trying

A last piece of advice about communications is that it is important to be persistent and keep the communications flowing. Even the most persuasive messages may not have impact immediately and may take a long time to show effects. A message may persuade people to become ready to act, but they may not actually act until the right opportunity comes along. If groups of women are persuaded to abstain from drinking when pregnant, they may not get the chance to demonstrate that the message got through to them until the time when they actually get pregnant, and the effects of the persuasive message may not really show up until years later, when their children perform better in school and in confronting life's challenges than the children of their friends who were not persuaded to abstain.

Getting the Word Out Persuasively in Pink: Susan G. Komen for the Cure

Back in the 1970s, I served on an advisory panel to the National Cancer Institute and its Health Message Testing Service. This was a short-lived program that took mock-ups of public service announcements and advertisements encouraging healthy behaviors and put them through careful copy testing with the public, using the methods and facilities of a major marketing research firm to determine which messages should be fully produced and distributed and which should be discarded. Any not-for-profit organization could submit messages for free testing. Among the most difficult types of messages to design were those about breast cancer. It was hard to talk about breasts in ways that did not offend certain constituencies, and it was hard to determine what themes and appeals to use. If you tried to get women to do breast self-examination and obtain mammograms by scaring them about the risks of getting breast cancer, then the message would often backfire in that many women would view breast cancer as a death sentence and decide that they would rather not know that they had it. On the other hand, if you stressed the value of early detection because significant progress was being made in treating breast cancer, then that would sometimes backfire too, as many women would think that they had less to fear and could always get it taken care of "later," especially since they were not confident that they could detect a lump in their breast on their own.

Fast-forward 35 years and think about how breast cancer is viewed today. Large numbers of women in the United States, and more and more around the world, routinely do breast self-examination and obtain regular mammograms. And hundreds of thousands of women are breast cancer survivors—who in another era might not have lived—and they proudly spread the word about the importance of early detection, compassionate treatment, and research. There are many people and organizations that deserve credit for changing the public's attitudes and behaviors toward breast cancer, including First Ladies Betty Ford and Nancy Reagan, the Lance Armstrong Foundation, and the American Cancer Society, but no one has done more for preventing and treating breast cancer than Nancy G. Brinker, the founder of Susan G. Komen for the Cure. And this social entrepreneur has scaled her impact dramatically by being masterful at orchestrating effective communications, the vast majority of which employ the color pink.[12]

Brinker started the Susan G. Komen Foundation in 1982 (later rebranded as Susan G. Komen for the Cure) to fulfill a promise she made to her beloved older sister, who died of breast cancer at the age of 36. Nancy had a background in public relations and marketing prior to starting the Foundation, and she put it to good use in scaling her impact, regularly refining her approaches and layering on new communications tools as the years went by. Her own bout with breast cancer increased her resolve to do everything within her power to reduce how much women around the world suffered because of this horrible disease. The Komen group has now raised hundreds of millions of dollars for breast cancer research, while also doing a standout job through their over 100 affiliates of educating women about the disease and getting them to take preventive and curative actions.

Observing the communications approaches used by Komen through the years, one can see that the organization has used all three elements of the *Switch* framework to great benefit, whether they are trying to persuade potential sufferers, donors, volunteers, scientists, or public policy makers. They have "directed the rider" by doing things like providing women with clear recommendations about doing breast self-examination, getting regular mammograms, obtaining complete information about treatment options, being vigilant about getting needed treatment and care, and being supportive of sufferers and survivors of the disease (e.g., registering for and running in a Race for the Cure 5K).

All this has been companioned with themes and messages that are highly motivational and able to inspire behavioral effects like increases in mammograms, monetary donations, volunteer time, or political support. For example, at the Race for the Cure 5K events that are now held all around the world, there are numerous emotion-charged messages circulating, with people wearing shirts and signs indicating that they are running the race "in memory" of a loved one who died of breast cancer or "in support of" a breast-cancer survivor. There are also very visible groups of survivors, wearing some type of pink outfit and a bandanna to hide their loss of hair, who often run together or gather before and after the races in special tents where they are treated as honored guests. Indeed, the word "cancer" by itself, accompanied by the now-familiar pink ribbons and pink colors that can be cues themselves, arouses emotions in people, no matter whether it appears in an advertisement urging people to participate in a Komen-sponsored walk, race, or other fund-raiser or on a package of Yoplait Yogurt, where people are asked to send in their lids so that a donation will be made to Komen. Storytelling about breast-cancer survivors and their valiant battles, which can be incredibly motivating, also fill many of their communications, whether this is done in speeches and personal appeals or on websites or videos.

Efforts to "shape the path," making it much easier for people to engage in the desired behaviors, have taken several forms. Komen and others have exerted pressure for insurance coverage for mammograms, diagnostic tests, and certain forms of treatment. They have also supported the use of mobile mammogram units that can be parked in high-traffic community locations, making it easier for more women to get mammograms. And toll-free information lines have been established in partnership with the University of Texas Southwestern Medical Center. The facilitation of donations has been accomplished through websites and registration links that make it easy to make a donation or sign up for a race with a credit card, and marketing programs for the cause, like the one with Yoplait, have made it possible for consumers to combine buying and donating.

Brinker's first major marketing position was at the upper-crust Neiman Marcus Department Stores, and she learned from Stanley Marcus the value of tailoring marketing communications to different audiences. The Komen operation has taken this lesson to heart and does not try to sell the same thing in the same way to everyone. They sponsor running races for runners (or people who want to train to be runners), long-distance walks for walkers, bike rides for cyclists, and dance-a-thons for dancers. They have big fund-raising galas with polo matches (one of Nancy's passions) for the well-to-do, and they have school-based bake sales for young people. Their "think pink" messages appear everywhere, from all the signage and printed materials of American Airlines during Breast Cancer Awareness month in October to the uniforms of the National Football League teams and the signage at Panera Bread restaurants during the same time period.

It helps that most of Komen's underlying messages do not involve asking people to discontinue engaging in negative behaviors. They are able to frame most of their messages in positive terms, such as "early detection saves lives," "healthy eating and exercise can make a difference," and "supporting a survivor is rewarding." Moreover, they have recognized that building the self-efficacy of women should be an underlying message in everything they do. They have managed to change the mind-set of tremendous numbers of women from seeing breast cancer as something that is "bad luck" and a "death sentence" to something they can control, fight, and overcome if they take things into their own hands and do not allow the medical system to determine their fate.

With her background in marketing, Brinker knew the value of research for guiding communications programs. Research has supported many of Komen's decisions, from the choice of the color pink, to the selection of locations to house new affiliates, to determining which partners to engage with, to deciding about rebranding, to evaluating results. For example, a 2010 study found that awareness of Komen matched that of the American Cancer Society (83 percent).[13] Recently, some academic research has indicated that pink is not the best color for stimulating empathy and generosity, which, of course, would be a challenge to the Komen approach. It should be interesting to see if the organization heeds this research and gives consideration to making things less pink.[14]

Concluding Comments

Communicating to people about the value of your theory of change and getting them to alter their behavior in ways that favor your organization's mission and goals is extremely important for most organizations to be able to scale their impact. Whether you are trying to get people to discontinue a harmful behavior, such as drinking alcohol while pregnant, or to persuade people to donate, volunteer, or join your organization, the development of persuasive messages, along with determining the media to distribute them, deserves systematic research and persistent effort. Failure to communicate effectively, especially to targeted beneficiaries, can stop a scaling effort dead in its tracks, no matter how good a job the organization has done in building up the other SCALERS capabilities. Without a doubt, if the people you want to help are unable or unwilling to cease bad behaviors and commence good behaviors, then scaling will never happen.

CHAPTER 5

Alliance-Building: Creating Synergies with Others

The financial meltdown of 2008 and the subsequent recession have created difficult economic circumstances, and many people could cope better if they knew how to manage their money more wisely. In research I have done on financial literacy, I have learned that too many people do not understand how budgeting should be done or how credit cards, mortgages, monthly payments, and compound interest really work.[1] Without this knowledge, they make decisions that get them in over their heads in debt, becoming saddled with mortgages and car loans they can't afford or student loans they can't pay back. Many consumers just spend and spend some more, creating personal crises while also contributing to the creation of real estate bubbles, consumer credit bubbles, and student loan bubbles that can cause serious economic troubles if they burst.

Improvement in financial literacy is clearly needed, so that people can manage their money competently and with less distress. Improved literacy could also help to prevent the development of bubbles or allow them to deflate at a tolerable pace.

But higher levels of financial literacy have been very tough to achieve in the United States and all around the world. This is something that will require the ingenuity and collaboration of hundreds of groups and institutions approaching the problem in innovative ways. Unfortunately, research suggests that past financial education programs targeted toward teens and adults have failed to accomplish much. As a consequence, there are those who argue that more success might be achieved with financial literacy interventions if younger children are targeted with the programs. One of those people who believes in financial literacy programs for children is Jeroo Billimoria, a social entrepreneur who started a program called Aflatoun that provides financial education to thousands of children around the world. Billimoria has had notable success scaling the Aflatoun program and is now launching a new social entrepreneurial effort labeled ChildFinance that is trying to bring both financial education and financial opportunity (e.g., access to savings accounts) to children around the world.[2]

In creating Aflatoun and in her efforts to scale ChildFinance, Billimoria has emphasized understanding the ecosystem in which her organizations operate and using that understanding to form partnerships and alliances that can be leveraged to achieve scaling success. She realizes that creating financial capability and opportunity for children—and potentially, in the long-term, more financially savvy adult consumers—is not something that can be done by a single organization or small group of organizations. She is trying to create a collaborating social movement that will reform the whole financial system. I have learned much about the importance of alliance-building in scaling from observing Billimoria, and I will have more to say about her approach later in the chapter. I also give special attention to Aflatoun's strong capabilities at replicating at the end of chapter 7.

The alliance-building organization capability is defined here as:

> the effectiveness with which the organization has forged partnerships, coalitions, joint ventures, and other linkages to bring about desired social changes.

The alliance-building SCALER becomes especially important for achieving success at scaling in situations where the organization's theory of change involves leveraging other organizations to help produce desired results. It becomes even more important when the scaling effort commences at a time when the organization's ecosystem is weak on social capital, but has enough financial capital to support the improvement of that social capital. Building the competence of alliance-building, of course, requires that potential allies populate the ecosystem and are willing to entertain collaboration.

Leveraging Alliances

Competence at alliance-building can support your efforts to improve all the other SCALERS. Girls on the Run (discussed earlier) generates staffing support through alliances with Boys and Girls Clubs and YMCAs, which sometimes allow their paid staff members to volunteer as "unpaid" executive directors of local Girls on the Run councils. VisionSpring, which sells very inexpensive eyeglasses to poor people in the developing world, has improved its communicating by forming an alliance with BRAC, the giant microfinance, education, and health-care organization, which has its all-female network of community health workers selling VisionSpring products and services in Bangladesh and other countries.

The lobbying capability of the Campaign for Tobacco-Free Kids, which has combated youth tobacco use successfully in the United States, has benefited from alliances with the politically influential American Cancer Society and American Lung Association, as well as with the National Association of State Attorneys General. In the realm of earnings-generation, City Year, which deploys young people to do a year of community service in urban areas, has capitalized on a strong sponsorship relationship with Timberland—and relationships with distributors and vendors have helped the financial well-being of Fair Trade USA, which takes a small cut of the revenues created by the sale of Fair Trade certified coffee by businesses like Starbucks.

The replicating capability of Billimoria's Aflatoun program, which has now been offered in 75 countries, has benefited greatly from alliances created with microfinance organizations, credit unions, and banks like ING, Rabobank, and Citicorp. Finally, the Marine Stewardship Council has gotten a big boost to its efforts to stimulate market demand for sustainable seafood by the alliance it has formed with Walmart, which highlights the Council's certification label on its seafood products.

These examples should help make the point that going it alone, or with only superficial relationships with other organizations, is not a recipe for scaling success. Deep, trusting relationships are key. Let me now offer a few ideas on how to build such relationships. More extensive discussions of how to construct alliances and collaborations can be found in works by Jon Huggett[3], James E. Austin[4], and Shirley Segawa and Eli Segal.[5]

Finding Collaborators

A good starting place for improving your alliance-building capability is the ecosystem map discussed in chapter 2. Consider your resource providers and allies and rivals, and first assess whether there is the potential to deepen any of the relationships that already exist. Deepening an existing relationship can be a much more efficient way to leverage an alliance to support scaling than trying to build a new relationship. The expense of building knowledge and trust should not be as imposing. So if a corporate sponsor is providing you with financial support, can you persuade the company to increase their funding by presenting them with research evidence that their support is bringing them returns in the form of increased consumer patronage or easier recruiting of new management talent? For example, I know of a major consumer-products manufacturer that increased its support of a social service agency because the agency was able to show that a large number of Hispanic participants in a health education program sponsored by the company switched to the company's health-care product from a competing product that had been traditionally favored by Hispanic consumers.[6]

If getting more financial support from an existing relationship is not feasible, there still may be the potential of deepening the relationship by expanding the number of volunteers or the amount of pro bono work the company provides to your organization. I have seen Billimoria obtain great benefit out of the pro bono work that has been done for her ChildFinance initiative by consulting and law firms. Aside from the valuable advice this has provided, it has led several talented professionals to become deeply engaged with the ChildFinance effort, potentially leading to contacts that can help build other organizational capabilities.

In going beyond existing relationships to create alliances, one can scan current rivals and even bystanders to see if any of them have the potential to become productive partners. In evaluating prospects, a number of criteria should be used, but prominent among them should be the "fit" of the two organizations. There should be a fit between the values of the two, but, contrary to what some might recommend, not necessarily between the missions of the two organizations. The two organizations must align with one another on issues such as being honest and transparent, taking care of employees, charging reasonable prices for services, and supporting each other's theories of change. But the organizations do not have to fit with one another in terms of mission. On the one hand, having an alignment on mission, where both organizations are committed to alleviate something like childhood malnutrition or age discrimination, can be helpful. Synergies can develop between the organizations, and economies of scale can potentially be achieved as more people are served by joint programs. However, consumers and donors can also see the alignment of missions as insincere and opportunistic. When an organization concerned with binge drinking or drunk driving aligns with a beer company to promote "designated driving," some people may question the purity of motives of the sponsorship. They may see it as a sneaky way for a beer company to encourage more drinking—recall the Road Crew story in chapter 2, where efforts to enable people to drink more were looked upon unfavorably in Wisconsin. What might seem on the surface to be a good fit between the organizations could backfire.

A better alliance might be what Samuel Adams Brewing Company is doing with Accion, the international microlending organization. They are working together on the Brewing the American Dream program to distribute $250,000 in loans of from $500 to $25,000 to small businesses in the food and beverage industry in the hope of stimulating economic activity and employment. Although the core missions of the two organizations may not fit that well on the surface (i.e., beer sales and economic development), many consumers could view this alliance as having purer motives than a designated driver alliance. Yes, there is a self-serving nature to what Samuel Adams is doing, but consumers might look favorably on the notion that the company could help itself and small businesses at the same time.[7]

Determining how consumers or other stakeholders will respond to alliances is not something that should be left to hunches or guesses. It is possible to conduct informative research studies to learn how people respond to different possible alliances. A variety of data-gathering techniques can be used to test various sponsors. People could be asked to rate directly how they feel about different pairings. This could be done by having people rank order pairings in order of preference or by completing a rating scale for each pairing. It is also possible to get this information more indirectly, using a technique called "conjoint measurement" to have people rank different profiles of a product, where there are profiles with high and low price, differences in packaging, variations in other attributes, and variations in sponsorships. If the profiles with one type of sponsorship are rated higher than those with another type of sponsorship, then that would mean that it would probably be wiser to pursue the former sponsorship.[8]

Research can also help in making decisions about branding and promoting alliances. Whether dual brands should be used or a new joint brand should be developed is something that can be determined with copy testing and experimental research methods. Through using survey panels that are willing to complete online questionnaires, you can obtain ratings of brand names and message themes. This can be done by having respondents compare names and themes and then rating or ranking them, or it could be done by exposing a randomly assigned group to one name or theme and another randomly assigned group to another name or theme—and then seeing which scores best in terms of attitude towards the organizations, intentions to donate or volunteer, intentions to patronize the organizations, or other measures of potential effectiveness.

Aligning Incentives

Once you have decided on your best prospects for deepening or commencing a collaborative relationship, the nature of the "deal" that you have with one another must be spelled out very clearly. For the key to a long-term relationship is identifying "win-win" possibilities, where both parties gain significantly from the alliance. Your social venture needs to net out obtaining more in value from the donations, earned income, volunteer help, or political support generated by the collaboration than the value of what is lost from spending time and effort collaborating—which could include the cost of your people's time (including the opportunity cost of that time) and the cost of allowing others to exert some control over your strategies and tactics.

At the same time, your collaborator must see the relationship as generating more than just an opportunity to feel good about supporting your social venture. If your prospect is a for-profit corporation, it must see the relationship as generating improvements in its corporate reputation, its sales revenues, or its ability to attract and retain employees, all with a net positive cash flow. Think about the net returns Home Depot obtains from its sponsorship of Habitat for Humanity. On the other hand, if the collaboration is with a nonprofit or government agency, they should not see the relationship netting out to be costing them more funds or effort than it is worth. They should see the relationship as making the "pie" bigger and giving all partners larger slices, not shrinking anyone's slice.

The "pie" could consist of donations, grant awards, earned income, volunteer time, or political accomplishments. Thus, the World Toilet Organization has accomplished much more in improving sanitation in many developing countries by getting 253 nongovernmental organizations (NGOs) and companies from 58 countries to advocate together than it could have if all the parties were advocating on their own. There is more political clout in having greater numbers of supporters.[9]

It is advisable to lay out the expectations for a collaboration in the form of a Memorandum of Understanding (MOU). This document should be specific about desired outcomes, roles, responsibilities, deliverables, deadlines, and financial arrangements. It should be something that lays out checkpoints at which progress toward mutually agreed-upon goals can be assessed, and there should be procedures stated for terminating the relationship if either party is displeased with what has transpired. An example MOU, created for a university-nonprofit-government alliance to fight asthma in the state of Michigan, is found in Exhibit 5.1.

Navigating Troubled Waters

Having a carefully developed MOU should mitigate the chances of serious disagreements or conflicts developing between partners. Yet problems can still flare up and, before turning to any termination procedures outlined in an MOU, steps can be taken to turn the relationship around. As with any partnership, including a marriage, transparency and communication are keys to resolving conflicts. Providing access to records, so that each party knows the costs and benefits experienced by the other, should be helpful, although that kind of information sharing could be inappropriate if two of the parties could be considered rivals and would therefore

EXHIBIT 5.1   MEMORANDUM OF UNDERSTANDING FOR THE COMMUNITY ORGANIZING PART OF COMMUNITY ACTION AGAINST ASTHMA

(1-22-01)

This is a Memorandum of Understanding between the University of Michigan School of Public Health, Detroiters Working for Environmental Justice (DWEJ), the Detroit Hispanic Development Corporation (DHDC) and Warren Conner Development Coalition (WCDC). For the purposes of this Memorandum, these agencies will be called "host agencies." This Memorandum of Understanding sets forth the working relationship of these organizations including their roles and responsibilities as a part of their involvement in the community organizing part of Community Action Against Asthma, hereafter called CAAA.

Philosophy/Principles: Throughout the term of this partnership, these partner organizations agree to abide by the philosophy and principles spelled out in the Detroit Community Academic Urban Research Center's "Community-Based Public Health Research Principles" adopted on July 24, 1996, agreed upon by the Community Action Against Asthma Steering Committee on December 16, 1998, and listed here:

1. Community-based research projects need to be consistent with the overall objectives of the Detroit Community-Academic Urban Research Center (URC). These objectives include an emphasis on the local relevance of public health problems and an examination of the social, economic, and cultural conditions that influence health status and the ways in which these affect life-style, behavior, and community decision-making.

2. The purpose of community-based research projects is to enhance our understanding of issues affecting the community and to develop, implement and evaluate, as appropriate, plans of action that will address those issues in ways that benefit the community.

3. Community-based research projects are designed in ways which enhance the capacity of the community-based participants in the process.

4. Representatives of community-based organizations, public health agencies, health care organizations, and educational institutions are involved as appropriate in all major phases of the research process, e.g., defining the problem, developing the data collection plan, gathering data, using the results, interpreting, sharing and disseminating the results, and developing, implementing and evaluating plans of action to address the issues identified by the research.

5. Community-based research is conducted in a way that strengthens collaboration among community-based organizations, public health agencies, health care organizations, and educational institutions.

6. Community-based research projects produce, interpret and disseminate the findings to community members in clear language respectful to the community and in ways which will be useful for developing plans that will benefit the community.

7. Community-based research projects are conducted according to the norms of partnership: mutual respect; recognition of the knowledge, expertise, and resource capacities of the participants in the process; and open communication.

8. Community-based research projects follow the policies set forth by the sponsoring organization regarding ownership of the data and output of the research (policies to be shared with participants in advance). Any publications resulting from the research will acknowledge the contribution of participants, who will be consulted with prior to submission of materials and, as appropriate, will be invited to collaborate as co-authors. In addition, following the rules of confidentiality of data and the procedures referred to below (Item #9), participants will jointly agree on who has access to the research data and where the data will be physically located.

9. Community-based research projects adhere to the human subjects review process standards and procedures as set

forth by the sponsoring organization; for example, for the University of Michigan these procedures are found in the Report of the national commission for the Protection of Human Subjects of Biomedical and Behavioral Research, entitled "Ethical Principles and Guidelines for the Protection of Human Subjects of Research" (the "Belmont Report").

Program Objectives to be Accomplished: The following are specific aims and objectives as stated in the grant as it was funded. CONEH refers to the community organizing activities of CAAA.

Specific Aim 1: To identify, prioritize and translate the relevant findings of the current CAAA data collection activities, together with proposed, additional CONEH data collection activities, to guide the implementation and evaluation of an expanded, community-wide intervention.

Specific Aim 2: To conduct and evaluate a multi-level community-based intervention in order to reduce exposure to physical environmental and psychosocial environmental stressors associated with asthma severity and exacerbations, and to strengthen protective factors (e.g., social support, community capacity) that may modify the effects of these stressors.

Specific Aim 3: To examine whether the conducted multi-level, community-based intervention enhances the effect of an intensive household intervention on the health and well-being of children with asthma and their caregivers.

Specific Aim 4: To increase community awareness and knowledge of factors associated with the environment and asthma through the dissemination of research findings to community residents in ways that are understandable and beneficial to the community.

Dates for this Memorandum of Understanding: The grant project period is from 9-18-2000 to 7-31-2005. This memorandum is intended to cover the entire grant period.

Responsibilities of the University of Michigan, School of Public Health:

1. Actively support the CAAA partnership.
2. Participate in the CAAA partnership through membership in the Steering Committee. Communicate with the Steering Committee members regarding administrative and programmatic issues related to the community organizing project in Detroit.
3. Provide overall program oversight.
4. Collect data, conduct preliminary analyses of existing and new data, and provide feedback to all partners and to staff as appropriate.
5. Provide financial and programmatic reports to the funder, NIEHS (National Institute of Environmental Health Sciences).
6. Serve as a point of contact with NIEHS.
7. Assist in the staff hiring process.
8. Develop and conduct an orientation to the project for partners and staff.
9. Work with the community organizers and administrative assistant in planning and conducting community forums.
10. Provide co-supervision of community organizing staff with each of the host organizations.
11. Serve as the fiduciary agent for this project. Pay the bills, dispense funds (see "Financial Arrangement" for more details).
12. Assist in providing resources and technical assistance in activities supporting the design and implementation of assessment, data collection, and evaluation systems.
13. Assist in the dissemination of results to the community.
14. Ensure that there is ongoing communication between the host organizations and the University of Michigan by sharing information regularly and frequently.

Responsibilities of Detroiters Working for Environmental Justice, Detroit Hispanic Development Corporation, Warren

Conner Development Coalition:

1. Actively support the CAAA partnership.
2. Participate in the CAAA partnership through membership in the Steering Committee. Communicate with the Steering Committee members regarding administrative and programmatic issues related to the community organizing project in Detroit.
3. Develop and conduct an orientation to organization for all community organizing staff.
4. Provide co-supervision of Environmental Policy/Community Organizer and the Administrative Assistant with the University of Michigan School of Public Health.
5. Provide office space for staff assigned to organization.
6. Facilitate communication and linkages between organization and other community organizations and groups.
7. Provide 10% of a staff person's time to serve as the "Host Agency Liaison." The responsibilities of this person will include:
   - Participating in the hiring of the community organizing staff using a process to be approved by the CAAA Steering Committee;
   - Participating in an orientation to the overall community organizing project;
   - Providing an orientation and integration of the Environmental Policy/Community Organizer and the Administrative Assistant to the organization;
   - Providing co-supervision of the Environmental Policy/Community Organizer and the Administrative Assistant. This would include day-to-day supervision to ensure attendance and adherence to the agency's policies, and oversight and assistance in his or her conduct of day to day job responsibilities as per the job descriptions.
8. Assist in providing resources and technical assistance in activities supporting the design and implementation of assessment, data collection, and evaluation systems.

9. Meet deadlines to ensure that the reporting process for the grant is a timely one.

10. Participate in the process of analyzing and translating the data collected to guide the efforts of the community organizers.

11. At all times, assure that the community organizers are carrying out their responsibility to focus on the community, with the goal of seeking ongoing, continuous input from the community.

12. Assist in the dissemination of results to the community.

13. Ensure that there is ongoing communication between the host organizations and the University of Michigan by sharing information regularly and frequently.

14. Provide necessary training on an ongoing basis to community organizing staff and Administrative Assistant.

Financial Arrangements: Each of the community partners involved in the Community Organizing part of

CAAA: DWEJ, DHDC, and WCDC will receive funds from The University of Michigan, School of Public Health for services rendered as host agencies, as a part of this agreement. For year one, each agency will received $13,000. There will be a slight increase each year (e.g., $13,200 for year two, $13,408 for year three). These funds are for community field costs, which include:

Liaison – 10% x 3 locations $15,000
Facilities Rental x 3 locations 9,000
Community Organizing Activities x 3 locations 11,100
Field Ofc. Supplies 1,200
Copying, printing 900
Telephone 1,200
Postage, express mail 600

Total Community Field Costs $39,000 divided by three = $13,000 each

To obtain the funding, after staff is hired, each agency will submit an invoice for the first six months of the first year, or $6,500. An invoice for the second six months will be submitted five months later. It will take approximately one month from the time the University of Michigan receives the invoice for it to be processed and for the agencies to receive the funding. Agencies do not need to keep a detailed track of the expenditures as a part of this agreement. The University of Michigan School of Public Health will also provide a computer at a cost of no more than $2500 for each of the four staff persons hired.

Memorandum of Understanding Amendments:

The agreement shall be renewed annually by the signatories.

Termination of Memorandum of Understanding:

This agreement may be terminated by either party provided not less than thirty days (30) written notice of intent to terminate is given and an opportunity for prior consultation is provided. In the event of termination, accounts shall be reconciled as of the date of termination.

Signatures:

This Memorandum of Understanding is entered into on
_____(date)
(signatures)

_____ (for the University of Michigan, School of Public Health)

_____ (for Detroiters Working for Environmental Justice)

_____(for Detroit Hispanic Development Corporation)

_____(for Warren Conner Development Coalition)

Source: http://www.nucats.northwestern.edu/community-engaged-research/grants-workshops-and-training/arcc-seed-grants/MOU_examples.pdf be subject to accusations of sharing information to facilitate illegal collusive behavior under the antitrust laws.

Beyond providing information, keeping lines of communication open and not letting concerns fester, should reduce the chances that disputes will boil over into unpleasant conflict. Of particular importance is updating new personnel about the nature of relationships so that they don't begin to distrust the partners because of lack of familiarity. Still, when one party feels like there has been a shift in the benefit/cost ratio it is receiving from a partnership—and the other party is not prepared or able to do anything to rectify the situation—then it may be time to terminate the partnership and explore other collaborations. This could happen, for example, because a corporate sponsor has had disappointing financial results and cannot afford its former generosity, or it could happen because the social venture is unable to deliver on the increase in sales it was supposed to bring to a sponsor through making it easier for consumers to choose brands that produce social and environmental benefits.

Engaging Other Players

A key element in producing productive alliances is the encouragement of deep engagement by the funders, employees, members, customers, and regulators of the various partners. I have seen this work especially well with Billimoria's ChildFinance effort. Instead of just asking managers of financial institutions, researchers, educators, lawyers, regulators, and others to simply donate a check to her cause or volunteer to teach a financial management class to children, she has recruited dozens of people to work on multiple "working groups" to formulate strategies for completing tasks that are needed to achieve success for her cause. She has several working groups of 20 or more people each dedicated to tasks like a) formulating the overall strategy, b) identifying needed regulatory changes, c) generating research to demonstrate that financial literacy and inclusion helps children, and d) refining the educational interventions. Each of these working groups has had two meetings of two days each during 2010–11, and the meetings are jammed full of heated discussions and consensus-building, all facilitated by Billimoria and her enthusiastic staff (and an occasional pro bono consultant). These meetings have generated enormous enthusiasm and interest in what ChildFinance is trying to accomplish, and already several of the working group participants have been able to obtain stronger commitments to the cause from their employers or institutions. This kind of face-to-face engagement truly helps to create deep, trusting relationships.

Alliance-Building for Building Playgrounds: KaBOOM

KaBOOM builds playgrounds in less advantaged neighborhoods and encourages children's play through advocacy and other programs.[10] The theory of change of the organization encompasses the following goals:

- construct innovative, kid-inspired play spaces, using a community-build model that improves the well-being of the children they serve as well as the neighborhoods in which they live;
- share the knowledge and tools needed for anyone to find, improve, and/or build playgrounds on his or her own;
- build a broad movement driven by research, analysis, policy, and community engagement; and

- the impact will be:
  - healthier, happier, and smarter children
  - greener cities
  - better schools
  - stronger neighborhoods

So building playgrounds is a means to an end, not an end in itself.

Since 1996, founder Darell Hammond and his colleagues have built over 2,000 playgrounds throughout the United States, transforming the lives of the children that use them, as well as the lives of the planners, sponsors, and volunteers that worked on building them. Moreover, new policies supporting the development of play areas have emerged in numerous cities because of KaBOOM's advocacy work, which includes providing free online tools to guide community-organizing efforts (and also playground builds). KaBOOM's success at scaling can be attributed to numerous factors, including a dedicated staff, insightful leadership, effective communications, and detailed guides for building the playgrounds that facilitate replication.

But what really stands out to me as a driver of KaBoom's scaling success is their ability to form synergistic, productive alliances with other organizations and groups. They have developed community partnerships with schools, YMCAs, and Boys and Girls Clubs that have helped them design and build structures that meet community needs effectively. They have developed building partnerships with corporations that have provided volunteer labor and supplies to accomplish the building, usually in a single day that also serves as a team-building exercise for the companies. And they have developed funding and cause-marketing partnerships that generate donations to KaBOOM, such as one with Ben and Jerry's that produced a donation with every pint of KaBerry KaBOOM-flavored ice cream sold. Moreover, alliances and partnerships have been formed with groups like Marian Wright Edelman's Children's Defense Fund or Jill Vialet's Playworks to do advocacy work.

Hammond learned the value of collaboration early in life. One of eight children from a poor family, his single mother moved all of them into a group home when Hammond was four. At the Mooseheart Child City and School (outside of Chicago, Illinois), Hammond developed an appreciation for what teamwork could accomplish to help the less advantaged.

Later, when Hammond and his cofounder, Dawn Hutchison, were launching KaBOOM, they received an important financial and psychological boost from Sid and Bernice Drazin, the owners of a popular local hangout in the Adams Morgan neighborhood of Washington, DC, called the Comet Deli. This collaboration provided them with the equivalent of office space, as they operated for several months from the restaurant's tables, and also provided them with free mentoring about how to run a business (and often free food).

KaBOOM doesn't partner with just anyone, but rather puts considerable effort into finding the "right" partners. The organization learned lessons from early builds that ended up taking too long and frustrating too many people. Lessons were also learned from projects that were abandoned before they got too far, such as a project in Rwanda that was initiated at the request of First Lady Hillary Clinton that became just too complicated, too political (mainly in Rwanda), and too risky to KaBOOM's reputation to pursue. So instead of trying to please all communities that come to them wanting playgrounds—or all companies that want to provide volunteers and benefit from the team-building experience—KaBOOM asks all potential partners to "apply" for the opportunity to work with them. They have established a set of criteria that they use to screen applicants, and they are careful to avoid relationships that could create conflicts over values and/or problems for KaBOOM's reputation. For example, if a corporation wants a playground built in less than four months, they will turn the project down, since such a rushed effort would become more like a transaction than a transformational experience.

Whether the partner is a community organization, corporation, or government agency, the KaBOOM leadership is extremely cognizant of aligning incentives and having every partnership create significant payoffs for the partner, not just KaBOOM. They want their community partners to get an exciting place for children to play and an opportunity to build community spirit and hope for additional change. They also typically ask the local community to put up 10 percent of the cost of a build so that the locals are invested in the project's success. At the same time, they want their corporate partners to benefit from having happy and team-playing employees who have worked on the builds, as well as from having greater sales from consumers that choose them over competitors because of the support being provided to an admirable cause like KaBOOM.

Companies like Home Depot, Target, State Farm, Kraft Foods, and Kimberly-Clark have found their experiences with KaBOOM to work well for team-building and attracting customers, and they are quite willing to continue paying for these benefits. Indeed, these relationships have gone so well that KaBOOM can cover much of its operating expenses with this type of earned income. They ask companies to pay roughly 90 percent of the cost of a playground, along with planning the project and showing up on build day with 100 volunteers. They can cover most of the rest of their expenses through the sales of playground plans and parts, and also consulting services to schools, government agencies, and corporations, some of which is done through their Imaginary Playground subsidiary.

Hammond and his colleagues are very conscious of having systems and approaches that can be replicated easily, which helps to lower costs while still keeping the quality of the structures and the experiences high. As part of this, they have developed standard agreements that lay out what the expectations and duties of each party will be. For example, community partners are required to sign a contract that states their agreement to insure and maintain the playground for its life. This has helped the relationships develop more smoothly, and conflicts and misunderstandings have been minimized.

Last, it is clear that engagement at a deep level with numerous people from its partner organizations is an important element of all KaBOOM's alliance-building. Though there is standardization and an emphasis on efficiency, the "people" aspect of making these builds successful is not shortchanged. As mentioned, they try to create "wins" for everyone involved with each build. Moreover, giving people great experiences generates excellent word-of-mouth advertising, and this drastically reduces the need to spend money on advertising and marketing designed to attract new neighborhoods and companies.

Concluding Comments

Going it alone may be an approach that works for certain business entrepreneurs, such as those who have developed some type of intellectual property and seek to harness all the profits from that property for themselves, fearful that any alliances could lead to the stealing of ideas or know-how and rob them of future financial returns. In the social sector, achieving social change—not financial gain—is generally prominent in the minds of social entrepreneurs, and this can often be done more rapidly, efficiently, and effectively if major collaborations are formed. The individual social entrepreneur may have to share some of the "glory" with others when pursuing alliances, but this is a price that most are willing to pay to achieve their desired social impact. In some cases, this may mean sacrificing short-term benefits for long-term gain, as investments must frequently be made in building deep, trusting relationships that do not bear fruit overnight. But like the instruction that must be given to people in financial literacy programs, it is often better to sacrifice short-term gain for greater long-term payoffs.

CHAPTER 6

Lobbying: Using Advocacy to Create Social Change Opportunities

North Carolina, where I have lived for decades, is a tobacco state. Tobacco farming, manufacturing, and distribution were mainstays of the state's economy in the past, and local leaders and politicians looked upon anything that ever so slightly threatened the prosperity or reputation of the tobacco industry with intense disfavor. But times have changed. For example, the city of Raleigh, the state capital, recently passed an ordinance banning smoking in city parks. An action like this was unimaginable in North Carolina a few years ago.

What turned the tide against tobacco in North Carolina and around the country? Many factors have come into play, including antismoking media campaigns from public health agencies, as well as health education programs in schools. Yet, what probably had the greatest impact on opinions about tobacco and tobacco usage were the advocacy initiatives of the antitobacco organizations, which filed lawsuits and lobbied for new laws and regulations governing tobacco. Groups like the Campaign for Tobacco-Free Kids were highly successful in encouraging and mounting lawsuits against the tobacco industry, which eventually led to huge fines being levied against the tobacco companies. These fines forced the companies to raise their prices, which had the beneficial effect of reducing demand for cigarettes, especially from young people. These groups also spearheaded efforts to encourage "sting" operations to catch retailers who sold tobacco to minors—and that helped reduce the availability of tobacco to teens. Another victory for these organizations came with the passage of laws banning indoor smoking.

The lobbying organization capability is defined here as:

> the effectiveness with which the organization is able to advocate for government actions that may work in its favor.

Lobbying—or, more accurately, advocating—may become a highly important competence to develop to scale impact when the organization's theory of change recognizes that only so much can be accomplished with innovative services, clever persuasion tactics, or deploying talented people, and that some type of public policy action is needed to make change occur. Implementing such a change theory will be easier if the organization already has accumulated ample political capital. But if that capital is not there, then it must be cultivated and utilized.

The goals of lobbying and advocacy can be varied. One goal can be the passage of new laws and regulations that will help achieve desired social changes. For example, Jeroo Billimoria's ChildFinance initiative, discussed in the last chapter, is trying to get banking laws changed in many countries to permit children to have access to safe, secure savings accounts and other financial services.

Another goal can be to achieve stronger enforcement of existing laws and regulations either by persuading policy makers to allocate more funds to enforcement or by supporting lawsuits and legal actions that will prompt courts to rule in favor of stronger enforcement. The Campaign for Tobacco-Free Kids primarily pursues this type of goal.

Still another goal could be to get public policy makers to allocate larger budgets to certain social programs. YouthBuild, a program that teaches disadvantaged youths skills in the construction trades, while also encouraging them to complete high school, has had many years of success in lobbying the US Congress to provide YouthBuild grants to disadvantaged communities. This work has helped the program grow to serve 273 sites in 45 states, replicating their initial success in New York City.[1]

Finally, a social venture may simply want government approval to pursue its theory of change. This can sometimes become an insurmountable obstacle. The otherwise successful Benetech Corporation, run by Jim Fruchterman, which has developed and marketed technologies to help the handicapped and the poor, was thwarted in its attempts to introduce a new land-mine detection technology in Africa. They were unable to navigate around numerous political obstacles that arose in their path. These obstacles were due to a lack of cooperation from the Defense Department and Congressional leaders. As Fruchterman put it:

> This project was one where political issues came to the fore, and we were not effective in addressing them. We were unfortunately trying to get government assistance during an administration which was fighting an ugly war in a distant land. The DoD [Department of Defense] wasn't feeling particularly humanitarian, and was protective about explosive technology. In hindsight, our timing was poor.[2]

Building Advocacy Capabilities

While it is important to acknowledge that there is considerable overlap between developing organizational capabilities in lobbying/advocacy and improving capabilities in communicating and alliance-building, the topic of lobbying (or advocating) is deserving of separate discussion, highlighting some special skills that need to be cultivated to build this capability. Effective advocacy includes the development and distribution of persuasive messages, as well as the forming of coalitions to create more political influence, but it also includes becoming skillful at:

- developing knowledge about legislatures, regulatory agencies, and the courts;
- acquiring intelligence about competing advocates;
- conducting research on the causes and consequences of the social problem;
- conducting research on potential remedies for the social problem;
- monitoring public opinion;
- playing politics and;
- supporting lawsuits and other legal actions.

Brief commentaries about how to develop each of these skills follow.

Developing Knowledge

Depending on the cause you are promoting and your theory of change, you may need to learn a lot about how legislative bodies, regulatory agencies, or judicial forums operate and make decisions. In many countries, acquiring this knowledge can be daunting, as the number of governmental bodies involved with a particular problem area, and the variation in the rules and procedures of those bodies, can be enormous. Take, for example, the problem of obesity in the United States. The government "players" that deal in some way with that problem include the Department of Agriculture (which supports some growers more than others, while also encouraging healthy eating), the Food and Drug Administration (FDA) (which deals with labeling), the Federal Trade Commission (which deals with deceptive health claims in advertising), the Centers for Disease Control (which promotes healthy eating and physical activity), local school boards (which can control what's offered in cafeterias and vending machines, as well as how much physical education is required), local boards of health (which inspect eating establishments), and so forth. An organization like the Washington, DC-based Center for Science in the Public Interest, which is committed to reducing obesity through advocating for public policy changes, must be knowledgeable about the workings of all these bodies. Their staff has strived for years to understand food politics. Sometimes knowledge like this can be obtained by hiring outside experts and lobbyists or by teaming with other organizations. But often it will be necessary to assign talented staff to the task of studying the political landscape.

Acquiring Competitive Intelligence

There is typically little consensus about how to mitigate any given social problem. Some people think the solution to violent crime is gun control; others think it is to make concealed weapons available to all. Some people think the solution to drug abuse is legalization of marijuana (and other products like methadone, which is perceived to encourage "harm reduction" rather than "harm elimination"); others think that stepping up the eradication of marijuana and cracking down on youth usage is the answer. Depending on what side you are on in these types of debates, it is important to understand what the other side is up to. What arguments and advocacy approaches are they using? Knowing this can help you in designing ways to thwart or counter their efforts. Sometimes you can acquire this information by regularly scanning the news media and by attending relevant conferences and events. Other times it might be helpful to "shop" or "become a member" of the competition.

Researching the Problem

A common need in an advocacy effort is to have data on "the facts" about the causes and consequences of a problem. Before public policy makers are willing to act in your behalf, they often want evidence about the severity or extent of the problem and whether you understand what is causing it. For instance, before policy makers would support putting warning labels on alcoholic beverages in the United States, alerting pregnant women to the dangers of drinking, they wanted evidence that fetal alcohol spectrum disorders affect a significant portion of the population and that scientists had found that even light drinking could be the cause. More recently, the organizations advocating for the recently passed Financial Services Consumer Protection Act, such as the Center for Responsible Lending (discussed further in chapter 7), were aided by the data they gathered on mortgage foreclosures and on how consumers are misled by credit card statements.

Having a research staff to generate needed advocacy data can be very helpful, but it may be a luxury most social ventures cannot afford. Sometimes, you can find relevant data fortuitously in the academic literature, and sometimes you can give consultants or academics small research grants to acquire data that might be useful to you. The academics, in particular, may be willing to "work cheap" because their main motivation may be to generate academic publications from the data. Of course, working with academics requires a willingness to allow them to publish results as they actually turn out, even if the positions of your organization are not supported by the data. You can decide to withhold the release of data generated by your own employees, but you cannot withhold data generated by an ethical academic.

Researching Remedies

The same options and warnings exist for generating data about how well certain policy actions can remedy a problem. Clearly, data showing a policy action "worked" in another locality can be extremely useful for persuading policy makers to adopt an action in their jurisdiction. Recognize, however, that conducting this type of evaluation research can be very difficult, as stressed in chapter 2 in the discussion about randomized controlled trials and other methods. And evaluations can find that a policy action failed or even backfired. Nevertheless, if you can acquire evidence that policy actions have produced desired results, it can be boon to your advocacy efforts. Organizations like Mothers Against Drunk Driving have been able use effectiveness data to help them to persuade state after state to adopt laws that, for example, require ignition interlocks for convicted drunk drivers, make DUIs felonies, and impose stiff penalties on drivers who refuse to take a breath test.[3]

Monitoring Public Opinion

Ultimately, most public policy makers must answer to the voting public, so it is useful to understand how those voters think and feel about problems and remedies. Is the public, at a minimum, ambivalent about the public policy actions you are seeking, or do many people dislike the actions you are trying to achieve? If you are advocating for controversial actions like laws to permit abortions or gay marriage, then you need to be sure that the citizens affected by such laws are clearly on your side and not about to create a firestorm of protest. In cases where strong resistance exists, you may need to hold back on advocacy for new laws and ordinances for a later time, with work proceeding instead on informing and educating the public about an issue. Focusing first on informing and educating may be advisable for even less controversial causes. For example, Fair Trade USA has introduced a new initiative labeled Fair Trade Towns, which is trying to spread the word about the benefits of buying fair-trade products throughout communities, using a grass-roots, volunteer-based approach in the hopes of eventually getting local government officials to require fair-trade products to be offered in local governmental facilities and schools.[4] This Fair Trade USA program is discussed further in chapter 10.

Keeping track of public opinion does not have to involve doing expensive and extensive polling with carefully selected and representative samples, the type of thing done by the Gallup organization for political elections. For a modest cost, it is possible to do short, online surveys of reasonably representative groups of citizens using the services of companies like Qualtrics and Zoomerang, which have prerecruited panels of consumers who have agreed in advance to complete surveys in exchange for receiving gifts. While the panel members may not match the population of interest perfectly, they are often a good approximation.

In addition to doing surveys, you can learn much about public opinion by monitoring newspapers, magazines, broadcast programs, blogs, forums, and other websites. While one has to be careful not to assume that people contributing to a forum or an online discussion are typical of any population, it is still useful to see trends in the coverage of certain topics or issues.

Playing Politics

Depending on your organization and cause, it may be necessary to inject significant resources into supporting certain political candidacies and lobbying. If your cause is charter schools, then you may need to help supporters of charter schools get elected to school boards. And if your cause is science and technology education, then you may need to lobby for larger state and local budgets devoted to university and secondary education science programs. While working with experienced political campaign strategists and lobbyists, who know how to "horse-trade" to get what they want, can help a great deal, even novice political operatives can achieve success if they are armed with persuasive data (see above) and well-crafted messages (see chapter 4).

Supporting Lawsuits and Other Legal Actions

When "going to court" becomes the strategy of choice for your organization to achieve certain objectives, it is important to have the right legal talent on your side. For many social ventures, paying high-priced lawyers their typical rates is out of the question. Fortunately, there are many lawyers and law firms that are eager to do pro bono work for what they perceive to be a good cause. Finding these people is not easy, but a systematic search using board members, legal directories, databases, and so forth can uncover candidates. For example, the Lex Mundi Pro Bono Foundation is a resource to tap for legal help in the United States (see http://www.lexmundiprobono.org).

Using Advocacy to Have an Impact:
The Campaign for Tobacco-Free Kids

This chapter began with a discussion of the Campaign for Tobacco-Free Kids. Let us turn back to this venture and examine its advocacy efforts more carefully.[5] The Campaign was started by Bill Novelli in 1995. Bill had been the cofounder and CEO of Porter Novelli, a major public relations firm headquartered in Washington, DC, which in the 1970s specialized in social marketing and public advocacy. He was the one who got me involved with the Health Message Testing Service discussed in chapter 4. Bill also has had leadership roles at CARE (as chief operating officer) and, after departing the Campaign, at AARP (as chief executive officer). He still serves as chair of the board of the Campaign.

Bill and his colleague, Matthew Myers, who leads the Campaign today, employed all the elements of effective advocacy discussed in this chapter. They commenced their work with a tremendous amount of knowledge about how Washington worked and a strong sense for the levers of power that might be exercised to change the way tobacco products were marketed and distributed to young people. And they added to the group's knowledge by hiring staff people who knew the ways of lobbying and filing lawsuits, and also understood how to shape public opinion. Over the years, they have added to this expertise, bringing on new professionals who have an understanding of state issues and international issues. Indeed, today they have an entire staff division devoted to state-level advocacy, in addition to new state-level offices for the organization. Moreover, there is now a well-staffed international division.

With a highly experienced team of people, "competitive intelligence" was readily accessible. Many of the Campaign's people had lived through numerous product-liability and deceptive-practices lawsuits involving the tobacco industry, so they had developed a strong understanding of the arguments, witnesses, evidence, and legal maneuverings the tobacco companies tended to employ. They knew that one of their biggest challenges in protecting kids from tobacco marketing practices was overcoming the industry's argument that as long as they were selling legal products, the advertising of those products was constitutionally protected free speech. There was also the issue of the required warning labels on tobacco products potentially absolving the companies of the "duty to warn" and protecting them from product liability claims. Still, there was an enormous amount of previously confidential information about the industry released in the various lawsuits, making it easier for the Campaign team to know what they were up against.

The experienced team also was well versed on what research has shown about (1) the effects of tobacco products on public health and (2) the effects of tobacco marketing practices on tobacco usage. They knew the research findings, as well as the researchers themselves, giving them access to a stable of potential expert witnesses to use in court cases. Some of this research, such as the work that found that consumers were misled into thinking "light" cigarettes were "safer," served as the basis for several successful lawsuits against the industry. (Lights are not safer, since smokers consume more of them and/or inhale them deeper in order to keep their nicotine levels up.)

The Campaign's team was also aware of research that showed that raising the price of tobacco products contributed significantly to declines in youth smoking rates, and this gave them a rationale for pursuing court decisions that would levy large monetary fines on the industry, as well as for lobbying for higher taxes on tobacco products. Anything that would force tobacco companies or their retailers to charge young people more would help the cause.

Keeping an eye on public opinion was certainly part of the Campaign's activities. Indeed, one of the reasons for their focus on "tobacco-free kids," as opposed to more general antitobacco positioning, was because research revealed overwhelming public support for protecting kids from tobacco marketing efforts. However, through tracking public opinion, the Campaign team also found that in certain states (like North Carolina) they had to pay particular attention to public concern for the plight of tobacco farmers. Finding ways of compensating farmers for lost income therefore became an element in the settlements and legislation the Campaign sought. The polls showed that the public supports keeping tobacco away from children, but many people did not want a side effect of that to become economic harm to farmers.

The Campaign pursues both legislation and lawsuits with the goal of reducing teen tobacco use. It works closely with other organizations and individuals, such as the American Lung Association, the American Heart Association, the American Cancer Society, the attorneys general of many states, and locally based youth advocacy groups that the Campaign has helped to organize. The Campaign and its allies have received their share of bumps and bruises in both the legislatures and the courts, but they have won more often than they have lost. Besides achieving higher taxes and fines, they deserve credit for helping to get the bans on smoking in most indoor locations and for making it very difficult for young people to buy tobacco products in retail stores.

Nevertheless, Novelli and Myers went through a very difficult time trying to get federal legislation passed that would give the FDA the ability to regulate tobacco in a way similar to how it regulates prescription drugs. In 1997 and 1998, they came close to getting such legislation passed, but failed in part because industry lobbyists persuaded members of Congress that it was unfair to pass such legislation without providing the industry with immunity from being held liable for their actions that took place before the law came into being. Had this bill succeeded, much higher fines (and tobacco prices) would have resulted than what came out of the subsequent Master Settlement Agreement between state attorneys general and the tobacco industry. Reflecting on this battle, Novelli states:

> Sometimes you can learn more from defeat than from victory. At the Campaign for Tobacco-Free Kids, we didn't stop—we reviewed and revised our strategies and kept going. We increased attention and support to the states to help them fight for money from the Master Settlement Agreement and to work for other state-level policies, like increased tobacco taxes and smoke-free public places. We improved our grassroots coordination and strength, reaffirming that social change is, in large part, generated by people at local levels. We built new partnerships, including expanded alliances with the tobacco growers. We redoubled our congressional lobbying and moved to support international tobacco control. Above all, we didn't change our aggressive, hard-charging style.[6]

Finally, in 2009, under the Obama Administration, a law was passed giving the FDA regulatory authority over tobacco and how it is manufactured, distributed, and marketed. Nevertheless, the industry and the Campaign remain embroiled in legal confrontations over issues like how graphic the warning-label pictures should be on cigarettes, or what the industry should be allowed to say about the health effects of newer tobacco products like snus and lozenges. Regardless, it seems clear to me that the advocacy efforts of the Campaign have scaled their impact on youth tobacco usage dramatically.

Concluding Comments

Although many see social entrepreneurship as an *alternative* to having governments engaged in solving social problems—avoiding much of the politics and bureaucracy that can hinder the effectiveness of government initiatives—the reality is that many social ventures cannot achieve their missions and goals without governments becoming deeply involved with what they are doing. Governments can provide a steady source of funding for a social venture, or they can enforce laws and regulations that can put a serious dent in a social problem. All the anti-smoking campaigns and warning labels in the world did not do much to reduce smoking in the United States. But when governments cracked down and reduced the accessibility of tobacco products to minors and eliminated indoor smoking, while also pursuing lawsuits through attorneys general, the result was a rise in the price of tobacco products, and significant reductions in smoking rates followed. Developing competence at lobbying and advocacy is not easy, but success in this realm can often be achieved with in-depth research, effective framing of messages, and the formation of alliances with pro bono attorneys and others. You can receive results without building huge organizations and networks, or governmental funding can help to build those organizations and networks if that is what is called for in your theory of change.

CHAPTER 7

Earnings-Generation: Attracting and Replenishing Financial Resources

S elf-Help is a marvelous organization, headquartered in downtown Durham, North Carolina, about two miles from my office at Duke University. Self-Help is a community-development financial institution that has done a whole range of things to help poor people in North Carolina and around the country, including providing mortgages for responsible but poor homeowners, spearheading the rehabilitation and redevelopment of downtown Durham, and successfully promoting the passage of laws against predatory lending. A key element that allows Self-Help to do all it does is their excellent management of their financial resources. They have developed steady and reliable revenue streams and, at the same time, have kept expenses low, partly by putting a limit on the salaries they pay any of their employees, including their top leadership. Through the use of careful screening tools in their loan origination activities, they have issued very few "bad" loans and mortgages, and therefore have generated a steady stream of income from these activities. They have also generated income from the credit unions they own and manage. Effective money management of the assets has also led to income.

The earnings-generation organization capability is defined here as:

> the effectiveness with which the organization generates a stream of revenue that exceeds its expenses

Earnings-Generation may be the most important capability for scaling, except in those situations where either (1) the organization's theory of change relies primarily on using political capital to change laws and regulations or (2) the start-up capital available to the organization is sufficient to carry it a long way. Most theories of change require ample sums of money to build capabilities in staffing, communicating, and so on, and (as discussed in chapter 1) a scaling effort is likely to be dead on arrival without a business model that creates a flow of revenues that exceeds expenses. That business model can be one that relies on sales of offerings, a profitable social enterprise or side business, cause-marketing arrangements, sponsorships, donations, grant funding, bond financing, or government budget allocations, but it must be a steady and reliable source of financial capital. The best approach for building earnings-generation competence will depend on the forces, trends, allies, and rivals found in the organization's ecosystem.

Note that there is considerable overlap between the earnings-generation capability and the stimulating-market-forces capability. The difference between the two is that earnings-generation is primarily concerned with how an organization can attract financial resources, while stimulating market forces is concerned with how the organization can put incentives to work not only to attract financial resources, but also to attract human, social, political, technological, and natural-resource capital.

Approaches to generate earnings run the gamut from those that rely primarily on beneficiaries to pay a monetary price for receiving benefits to those that rely almost completely on the generosity of donors to provide financial needs. All require an ability to develop productive relationships with other parties (e.g., customers, sponsors, grantors, donors). A single approach does not have to be used, and hybrid approaches often make sense. A quick review of potential earnings-generation approaches follows.

Doing Well and Doing Good Simultaneously

The most straightforward way for an organization to generate a sustainable level of earnings is to sell an offering to the people it is trying to help for a monetary price that generates margins that not only cover the variable costs of each unit that is being sold, but also cover overhead and fixed costs after a certain volume has been achieved. If economies of scale exist in producing and marketing the offering—meaning that larger volume can be achieved at a lower per unit cost—then that can enhance the flow of earnings dramatically and stimulate more rapid scaling. Microfinance originally grew because it had these qualities. Every loan that was "sold" generated a profit margin (i.e., interest), and as more were sold they became cheaper per loan to sell and service. Similarly, VisionSpring is trying to make money off each pair of reading glasses it sells—and as volume increases their cost per unit of manufacturing and marketing the glasses decreases—but this organization has not yet reached the point where they can cover overhead and fixed costs with the sales volume and margins they are achieving. VisionSpring still relies on other sources of funds like donations and grants to make ends meet.

The importance of achieving low costs in supplying products or services cannot be stressed enough. Expensive manufacturing or service-delivery approaches will typically be beyond the financial-capital capabilities of most social entrepreneurial organizations, and the customers of these organizations are often poor and unable to pay much for offerings. Keeping the drugs, therapies, medical devices, educational classes, conservation equipment, or certification program cheap and easy to access is usually necessary to allow significant portions of needy populations to obtain what they need at a price that still generates a sustainable profit for the organization.

An example of an organization that is embarking on a scaling effort that is built around the principle of keeping costs very low, but still selling to poor people at a profit, is Driptech. This for-profit company, started by a PhD student in mechanical engineering at Stanford University, has an innovative manufacturing process that can produce what is claimed to be "the best drip irrigation system for small-plot farmers—affordable, high quality, and easy-to-use." Driptech systems are priced at least 50 percent lower than the nearest competition, so that a small-plot family would be able to afford and purchase a Driptech system that would produce enough vegetables to increase their income. Furthermore, after buying this system, farmers should supposedly be able to recoup their initial investment in less than 6 months, leading to significant increases in income over the next 3 to 5 years, the lifespan of the product. Driptech has formed partnerships with major distributors in India and China, and it expects to achieve substantial growth very quickly.[1]

Cross-Subsidization

The ability to make a profit margin on each unit sold to beneficiaries, whether it be a loan, pair of eyeglasses, water filter, bed net, or contraceptive, should not be viewed as a license to charge people prices they really cannot afford for offerings. It can be argued that overcharging on interest is what has created a backlash against microfinance in countries like India, where timely repayment on microloans has recently gone from near 100 percent with many institutions to closer to zero today. Poor consumers have rebelled against paying interest in the 30 percent range and even higher.[2] Yes, getting higher prices can fuel more rapid scaling, but not if it causes the entire venture to implode.

However, if some people find it comfortable to pay more than others, it is possible to cross-subsidize the offerings provided to less-advantaged people with the profits earned from serving more advantaged people, thus creating financial sustainability for the organization in the process. A classic example of cross-subsidization is the approach that has been taken by the Aravind Eye Hospitals in India. Their most common offering is cataract surgeries, and they have developed procedures for completing those surgeries safely, inexpensively, and effectively. All patients, no matter what their financial circumstance, receive the same surgical attention by the same doctors and nurses. However, the organization has found that more wealthy patients are willing to pay more for the ability to spend their waiting times before and after surgery in more luxurious rooms. Hence, the group uses the profits made from the more "plush" surgeries to subsidize and lower the cost of the surgeries for the poor. In a similar vein, many educational and training programs charge greater tuition and fees to the more affluent, while providing "need-based" scholarships to those with lesser ability to pay.

Generating Earnings from Nonbeneficiary Markets

Another way to subsidize the delivery of desired offerings to beneficiaries at low or zero prices is to develop successful side businesses or social enterprises. One approach to this involves developing a successful business that generates profits that benefit needy people in two basic ways: 1) by providing needed offerings to beneficiaries (e.g., therapy, treatment, training, housing assistance, food) and 2) by giving beneficiaries jobs in the enterprises. There are catering services, moving services, landscaping services, and so on that are paying for themselves in places like San Francisco, Chicago, New York, and Durham, North Carolina, while providing therapy and treatment to former drug abusers and convicts and at the same time also providing them with meaningful employment. Several of the organizations funded and supported by The Roberts Enterprise Development Fund (REDF) in San Francisco operate this way (see below),[3] as does Triangle Residential Options for Substance Abusers (TROSA) in Durham.[4] Another example can be found in the organization Specialist People, from the United Kingdom, which employs autistic people to test software for software developers. The attention to detail that autistic people are often capable of demonstrating can produce more effective and efficient software testing than can be done by other testers. Software developers can actually save money and get better results from patronizing Specialist People, which should lead to more sales for the social enterprise as well as more ability to help and employ autistic people.[5]

It is also possible to simply run a social enterprise that does not employ its targeted beneficiaries, instead focusing on generating as much funds as possible for its cause using whatever labor force is appropriate for improving earnings. AARP (American Association of Retired Persons), the organization that has successfully obtained numerous legal and economic improvements for older Americans, generates much of its funding from the advertising revenue of its widely read magazine, and it also receives a percentage of the revenues obtained by affiliated insurance companies that sell home, auto, and health policies. Riders for Health, a program in Gambia and other African countries that delivers patients and health workers to health clinics by operating a network of well-maintained motorcycles, has developed a social enterprise that takes tourists on exciting and educational motorcycle tours around these countries.[6] Dozens of other social entrepreneurial organizations generate funds by selling food, second-hand clothing and furniture, jewelry, artwork, and other offerings. Sometimes these offerings have been sourced from operations that pursue fair-trade practices that take good care of workers and the environment—and that can make these offerings more attractive to some segments of consumers who are interested in socially responsible consumption. But other times, attractive offerings can generate ample revenue without a fair-trade identification.

Cause Marketing and Sponsorship

An increasingly popular way for social-purpose organizations to generate revenue is to enter into a cause-marketing or sponsorship relationship with a consumer products company. In a sense, companies that participate in these relationships have decided that by alerting the public to their philanthropic endeavors, they might achieve benefits beyond any good feelings that managers might feel for supporting a good cause. Consumers may be more likely to choose a brand if the company is donating a percentage of every purchase, a share of profits, or some other significant amount to a cause they appreciate. Moreover, employees may be more attracted to working for or staying with companies that support causes they appreciate. So the Hole in the Wall Gang Camps for children with life-threatening illnesses, started by the late actor and activist Paul Newman have grown because of their strong affiliation with Newman's Own food products. This highly successful company gives 100 percent of its profits to charity, with the bulk of it going to the camps, and many consumers buy Newman's Own products because of a desire to help the camps. The products are of high quality and are priced competitively, so consumers do not have to sacrifice anything to favor Newman's Own brands. It is a win-win-win situation, with the company, the cause, and consumers all benefiting.[7]

In a similar vein, City Year and its programs to revitalize inner cities using the help of City Year corps members, have gained from sponsorship from the apparel company Timberland. Other highly visible cause-sponsor relationships have been the Lance Armstrong Foundation and Nike, Habitat for Humanity and Home Depot, and The Global Fund to Fight AIDS, Tuberculosis and Malaria and Product Red (marketed by The Gap, Hewlett Packard, Apple, and others).

Key to arranging and sustaining a cause-marketing or sponsorship relationship is the accumulation of evidence that consumers and/or employees are likely to (or have already begun to) favor companies over competitors because of the relationship. For example, Susan G. Komen for the Cure (see chapter 4), which raises money for breast cancer research partly by conducting Race for the Cure 5K races all over the country, worked a number of years ago with one of their major sponsors, Ford Motor Company, to determine consumer reactions to the sponsorship. They found that people who had participated in the race were much more likely than those who had not participated to go to a Ford dealership and test-drive a Ford automobile. No wonder Ford has continued to sponsor the race series for over 17 years.[8] While conducting such a study might not be affordable to some social ventures, even qualitative and anecdotal evidence about how a cause relationship has influenced consumers or employees can be extremely valuable.

Attracting Investments, Grants, and Donations

The kind of evaluation data accumulated by Komen and Ford, but more focused on whether the interventions of the social venture have actually caused the mitigation of a social problem, is an important ingredient for attracting philanthropic funding and socially oriented investments (which are now often labeled as "impact investments"). Beyond having metrics and measures to help make your case to grantors/donors/investors, you need to be well organized for fund-raising and have the research data and talent necessary to succeed at it. Data on donor/investor habits, desires, interests, and affiliations can be extremely valuable for forming connections and crafting appeals. Furthermore, employing people or utilizing board members and volunteers who are adept at writing case statements and grant proposals, tracking and analyzing prospects, doing face-to-face selling of your organization's benefits, and stewarding previous supporters is terribly important. The organization's leader or founder will have to do much of the face-to-face selling, as prospects typically like to "personify" an organization—and, frankly, there are numerous highly charismatic leaders of social ventures that you may have to compete with, and if you don't have such a leader, some donors may not give you the time of day.

One of the benefits of doing face-to-face selling is that it provides an opportunity to probe and clarify the true motives and desires of the grantors/donors/investors, since it often is not possible to determine what a foundation officer or wealthy individual might find compelling about your organization. Reading requests for proposals, mission statements, priority announcements, and so forth can be revealing and helpful, but it may not allow you to detect how your organization is perceived (or misperceived) by the grantor/donor/investor and how those perceptions match up with what they see as the characteristics of their ideal or preferred grantee or funding recipient. A number of studies have been done on "why people give," and it is useful to review them before you approach a grantor/donor/investor to provide ideas about what questions to ask. For example, Hope Consulting recently completed a set of studies about motives for doing impact investing that produced some provocative results. Motives that were frequently cited included a desire to respond to a natural disaster and a desire to accomplish as much as possible with one's money (which is perceived to be an argument for international giving).[9] In sum, fund-raising is both a science and an art requiring incredible dedication and perseverance.

Achieving Financial Sustainability: REDF

It is hard to identify a single social entrepreneurial organization that employs all the many different ways of generating revenues discussed in this chapter. But there is an organization of organizations, REDF, that has directly or indirectly used virtually all the approaches. This innovative venture philanthropy organization from San Francisco has used a variety of strategies to fund its core operations, and it has financed and consulted with its many nonprofit portfolio organizations as they have deployed additional earnings-generation strategies.

REDF was originally called The Roberts Enterprise Development Fund, serving primarily as a venture philanthropy initiative of George Roberts, a cofounder of the influential global leverage buyout firm Kohlberg Kravis Roberts & Co. (KKR). An earlier incarnation of REDF was the Homeless Economic Development Fund (HEDF), which operated from 1990 to 1996 with a mission to help the homeless in the Bay Area find jobs and shelter. REDF was launched in 1997, and it had a broader focus of creating job and career opportunities for people facing great difficulties finding employment, such as the handicapped, the previously incarcerated, or the recovering substance abuser. The organizations it has supported are virtually all "social enterprises" in that they sell goods and services like food, janitorial services, trash hauling and recycling, and property and landscaping maintenance to generate revenues, and they then feed the funds back into providing salaries, job training, and therapy to unemployed and underemployed populations. The expenses these organizations cannot cover through their earned income activities are covered by grants, donations, and investments made by REDF and others. REDF invests as if they were venture capitalists, providing equity capital and technical assistance in executing plans for growth and in measuring results.[10]

Some of REDF's portfolio organizations have included:

- Green Streets, which manages recycling and composting for businesses, homes, and multifamily properties in San Francisco for negotiated fees. They help their clients lower their trash bills, reducing waste by an average of 40 percent at the places they serve.[11]
- Buckelew Programs, which focuses on providing job training and jobs for people suffering from mental illness and addiction in northern California. Their two major social enterprises are Blue Skies Coffees and Teas (with cafés) and Blue Skies Cleaning Services.[12]
- Solutions SF, which provides lobby staffing, building maintenance, and bed-bug remediation for multifamily properties, employing hundreds of formerly homeless people and paying them a fair wage and health benefits.[13]

REDF has also made a name for itself as a disseminator of knowledge about social entrepreneurship. They have been especially active in pushing for better metrics for evaluating social ventures, and their staff has written extensively about Social Return on Investment (SROI).

Many of REDF's portfolio organizations have been able to be social enterprises that "do well and do good" simultaneously. Organizations like Green Streets are able to earn a steady revenue stream from business clients who willingly pay to have someone sort recyclables for them or dispose of solid waste properly. Revenue is therefore generated while the group also helps to keep the environment clean, and needed job skills and steady jobs are created too.

Other REDF organizations contribute to their own financial sustainability by doing cross-subsidization. For example, People's Harvest charges higher prices for transporting and marketing locally grown, healthy foods to hospitals and schools in wealthier neighborhoods than they do for poorer ones, allowing the former areas to subsidize the latter areas, while still providing everyone with healthier eating options.[14]

Of course, many of the social enterprises under REDF's umbrella are essentially revenue-generation propositions, and the products or services they sell are not directly socially beneficial. So when Blue Skies Coffees and Teas (a Buckelew operation) sells baked goods, the products being sold are doing little to resolve a social problem, but the money generated can help with job training and therapy at Buckelew—and the local bakery that supplies Blue Sky can employ more people too.

REDF itself has used cause-marketing approaches, such as the arrangement they have with Rickshaw Bagworks. Rickshaw sells a stylish "Charity Messenger" bag for toting things around while on bicycle or foot, of which a significant percentage of the proceeds go to REDF.[15] Presumably, this association with a good cause helps Rickshaw sell more bags. And REDF also urges businesses to buy the products and services of its portfolio organizations, publicizing those that do on its own website and encouraging the purchasers to do the same. So, for example, Numi Organic Tea advertises that it uses the contract labor of REDF portfolio member Community Gatepath, an organization that employs people with disabilities, to pack its Assorted Boxes and Gift Packs, and this likely helps them sell more tea.[16]

REDF has also succeeded in attracting grants from other foundations and governments at all levels. By 2011, the organization had received $6 million from the Social Innovation Fund—which REDF had to match twice with outside funds to get to a total of $18 million for its portfolio organizations. This high-profile funding would not have been possible without REDF being able to document the effectiveness of the programs it supports using rigorous evaluation methods. This documentation and the generally high profile that REDF has had in the social entrepreneurial world, serving as an exemplar of how to scale impact and document results, has certainly also helped them in attracting funds from impact investors and other private donors. Commenting on their external grant-seeking and fund-raising, Carla Javits, president of REDF, remarks:

> When I first came to REDF in 2008, we were focused on our work in the SF Bay Area, and influenced others mostly through our publications, tools, speaking, etc. In those first few years, I met with people at many foundations to inform them about what we had done, what we had learned, and garner their advice about the work itself, our strategy, and also how to engage with them— particularly given that REDF was founded by an individual of high net worth as part of his foundation, and, with his continued support, was now trying to attract the interest of other funders. We learned that we needed to be able to shape the message around the people that each foundation is interested in; and/or the cost

effectiveness and impact of our work; and/or the effort to "scale" social innovation. The imprimatur of the Social Innovation Fund was really helpful in building greater momentum, as was our strategic decision to focus on both California expansion, and developing a replicable national model.[17]

Finally, REDF has cultivated private donors very effectively by staging highly engaging and informative fund-raising events. For example, in September 2011, they staged their third annual Social Enterprise Benefit and Expo at the Bently Reserve Conference Center in San Francisco, attracting over five hundred people. Quoting Javits again:

> The focus was two-fold: (a) The Stuart G. Moldaw Step-Up Award given to outstanding social enterprise employees (Stuart was on REDF's Board—a major philanthropist and businessman who also was behind the start-up of Ross Stores and Gymboree); and (b) a business Expo that featured 13 of the organizations that are or have been in REDF's portfolio. We provided as an incentive "prizes" to all those who visited a certain number of booths. On average, those attending visited four booths. The purpose was to learn more about the enterprises, and also to provide them with business leads and other kinds of support that we detailed. It was a very high energy and successful event.[18]

REDF has also convened more informal gatherings, sometimes with speakers, to raise funds.

Concluding Comments

The earnings-generation capability is typically a necessary but not sufficient condition for scaling social impact. This capability may be needed in order for the other SCALERS capabilities to improve, although these other capabilities will often have a reciprocal relationship with earnings-generation.

Good staffing, communicating, alliance-building, lobbying, replicating, and stimulating market forces can all enhance earnings-generation. The variety of approaches available for generating earnings is numerous, and what works for one organization at one time may not work for the same organization at another time or for a slightly different organization. Thus, Self-Help may at some point not be able to generate the earnings from mortgages that it once did, and may have to turn to other approaches. Other community-development financial institutions may have to rely more on grant-funding or donations. Whether you intend to attract earnings through a profitable social enterprise or side business, cause-marketing arrangements, sponsorships, grant-funding, donations, or some other approach, it is important to be systematic and research-based as much as possible. Charisma and selling skills can help in this realm, but obtaining and analyzing data on market opportunities, donor behavior, consumer and employee decision-making, program effectiveness, and other matters can improve earnings-generation substantially.

CHAPTER 8

Replicating: Creating Evidence and Systems to Support More of the Same

The Citizen Schools program recently was introduced in Durham, North Carolina. Started in Boston in 1995 by Eric Schwarz, the initiative serves low-income, middle-school children in after-school programs supervised and taught by a mixture of paid staff and volunteers. The lessons cover topics like "College to Career Connections" and "Student Success Habits." Rigorously conducted evaluations of the program's interventions have found that students who have gone through the Citizen Schools program are 20 percent more likely to graduate from high school than a control group of comparable students who have not received the interventions. These data have given donors, funders, and potential host schools confidence that the program works, and with the development of a "playbook" or system that new schools could easily understand and adopt, the program is scaling rapidly. There are now seven states that run Citizen School programs, serving thousands of children, and evaluation results continue to report strong positive results.[1]

The replicating organizational capability is defined here as:

the effectiveness with which the organization can reproduce the programs and initiatives that it has originated while documenting persuasively that they have accomplished their objectives.

The capability of replicating effectively will be an important driver of success in those situations where scaling impact also involves growing an organization's size and/or reach. If more service providers, service locations, and distribution points are needed to have an impact on more people, then replicating will be essential. But even where the primary theory of change revolves around seeking public policy changes, replicating can come into play, as the ability to repeat successful advocacy efforts in different states or countries may be important.

Typically, replicating will be more influential for scaling impact when the beneficiaries an organization seeks to serve are relatively homogeneous. A replication system can potentially take advantage of economies of scale when similar service packages or products will be effective in different markets or areas. Those scale economies may not be there when customized services/products are required, and this may suggest that other SCALERS may be more important for achieving scaling success. At the same time, the intent to utilize certain technologies to help match people and/or organizations or to improve logistics may indicate that replicating is a more important driver. Part of building the replicating capability may also involve the acquisition and/or replenishment of technological skills, unless the organization is amply endowed with technological capital as it embarks on its scaling effort, which could mean that adding to its replicating capabilities through improving things like its information technology staff may only have minimal additional impact on scaling success.

Understanding What Works

To replicate effectively, you first need to understand what it is that should be replicated. This means conducting rigorous evaluations of what you have done in the past so that you can determine with confidence what the causes of previous successes have been. Are students graduating high school in greater numbers because of your after-school program, or because other factors have had greater influence on their success? Are malaria rates down because of your bed-net distribution efforts, or because of other improvements in mosquito control? Are more farmers earning a living wage because they have had access to your irrigation pumps, or because demand conditions have improved? As discussed repeatedly in this book, evaluation questions like these are very difficult to answer with precision, but you need to make efforts to isolate what is working well with your programs. You want to invest in replicating approaches that are documented to be working, not in ones that are producing disappointing results.

To be sure, it is never too late to get serious about evaluation. Even if you have not implemented the kind of evaluation design that allows you to say that your intervention has improved things over the way things used to be—or that your intervention has produced better results over recent times than alternative interventions (or than doing nothing)—you should commence taking the kinds of measures that will allow future comparisons to be made to how you are doing now or to how others are doing. Start doing regular tracking surveys of key stakeholders, start collecting data on website clickstreams or phone inquiries, and try to track whether the social problem you are seeking to mitigate is getting better or worse over time. Are fewer people living below the poverty line or spending time in hospital emergency rooms? Being able to point to the fact that the problem is getting better—even if you cannot say your intervention is responsible for the improvement—can be very good for mobilizing people and building the spirits of your staff and volunteers.

Besides showing you what to replicate, good evaluations can serve the added benefit of helping you attract the funding needed to replicate. As has been stressed before, funders are seeking this kind of accountability. However, pleasing and attracting funding should not be the primary reason for conducting evaluations—and using a hands-off approach that involves subcontracting an independent, outside evaluation firm primarily to placate funders, without becoming deeply engaged with the whys and hows of the evaluation, is short-sighted and can often be detected by funders. More than anything else, managers should undertake evaluations to provide them with guidance about the best interventions to use in the future.

Once you uncover what seems to be the key to your success in mitigating a social problem, you may find that it is something that can be deployed over and over again without building a lot of infrastructure, staff, and other capabilities. For example, if you have a good computerized matching algorithm for matching volunteers with volunteer opportunities, then the bottleneck for achieving scaling will not be your capacity for handling numerous matches, but rather, it will have more to do with your ability to attract individuals and organizations to sign up for being matched. Or if you have a production facility capable of producing at a low cost per unit a large volume of a product you are promoting (e.g., contraceptives, eyeglasses, irrigation pumps, water filters, toilets), then the replicating problem becomes more one of marketing and distributing the product, perhaps through allied distributors, rather than a problem of building a distribution or retailing network from scratch. Still, many organizations will need to build infrastructure and staff to replicate their successful programs, addressing issues such as those discussed below.

Creating the "Playbook"

Many organizations have developed curriculum guides, technical assistance guidelines, "how to" booklets or kits, webinars and training programs, games and simulations, and so on to support those who are trying to introduce a tested and effective program in new settings. This approach can eliminate the need for managers in new locales to have to "reinvent the wheel," giving them tried-and-true ways to address problems.

Girls on the Run has a curriculum guide that suggests what a volunteer coach should try to do in every after-school session of its 12-week program. The guide is tweaked and refined on a regular basis, based on tests conducted by the central office, and coaches are allowed to inject some of their own creativity into how they implement the program, but basically the Girls on the Run sessions on a given day in Raleigh, North Carolina, will be the same as the sessions done in Kalamazoo, Michigan. Similarly, BRAC has a guide for its elementary education programs in Bangladesh that allows these programs to be delivered with quality, but at a very low cost because they use primarily low-paid or volunteer teachers. Aflatoun's child financial-literacy curriculum has a guide, and it has been adopted widely, yet individual financial institutions adapt the curriculum to local languages, needs, and priorities (see more below). The Vision Entrepreneurs of VisionSpring all have guides (and training) to help them be more successful in local villages and neighborhoods. Information is provided on how to administer eye exams, manage inventory, and advertise their activities.

Having a playbook can help to ensure that the quality of offerings remains high and that the reputation of the venture is not damaged by having poorly run classes, exams, or fittings. Nevertheless, following the playbook strictly and creating a totally standardized offering in all locales may not be called for. Customization of offerings may be highly appropriate in certain situations. However, modifications of an offering to fit the unique needs of a locale should be done with caution, as damage can come to the entire system if one "outlaw" locale does something different and generates bad publicity for it.

Branching versus Affiliation

A way to avoid "outlaw" distributors of your offerings is by setting up branches of your original organization in different locales. Everyone in the branches works for the parent organization, affording you much more control over how they behave. Setting up an organization like this requires considerable financial and human capital in exchange for "control," and it might not seem worth the expense. Often, as much can be accomplished by forming alliances with affiliates, who will serve as the "face" of your organization in certain markets, but will not be working for you. They will work for independent entities, sometimes as franchisees that have a contractual relationship with your franchisor organization. They can be terminated as a franchisee if they engage in acts that are deemed detrimental to the whole system, which provides the ultimate control over them. Whenever an affiliate or franchise network is utilized, it is important to keep communications flowing through affiliates-only conferences, special websites, and regular conversations. Also, as discussed in the section on alliance-building, it is very important for all parties to have a clear understanding of the financial terms of the affiliation.

Both branching and affiliation have worked well for social entrepreneurial organizations, and one approach is not automatically better than another. Citizen Schools uses branching, as does Playworks, the program discussed earlier that provides recess programs for schools. However, Playworks has found branching to be an expensive way to replicate, as hiring talented employees to run programs in schools can be costly, and they are looking for other models to deploy. They are testing a "train the trainer" approach, which comes closer to being the kind of *dissemination* approach to scaling that was previously discussed. With this approach, schools that cannot afford the entire $55,000 per-year package that Playworks normally provides can instead contract for one of their training packages that a group of teachers or support personnel can attend. This can be done on the school site, and might cost as little as a few thousand dollars for a three-day "Recess Implementation" class. One school system in Stockton, California, sent 42 security guards to such a session and reported positive results.

On the other hand, Habitat for Humanity and Aflatoun, also discussed earlier, use the equivalent of franchising, with each locality being served by an independent organization that works with the parent organization. One of the characteristics of franchising is that an independent organization sells the products and services that the parent organization or franchisor has authorized all franchisees to sell. The independent franchisee must be financially sustainable on its own, and usually has to pay the franchisor a fee for being part of the system and sometimes has to buy products or services from the franchisor. This means that the financial capital required to become a franchisee may be substantial, and, in many less developed countries, this may make conventional franchising difficult to scale. As a consequence, "microfranchising" has caught on in the developing world, which provides microloans to franchisees to enable them to pay franchise fees, maintain inventory, and so forth. Living Goods is an organization that brings health solutions to the poor of Uganda using this approach.

The problem with microfranchising is that the franchisee is put in a demanding financial situation, making it difficult to really prosper and grow. An alternative approach that is gaining traction has been labeled "microconsignment," where products and services are put in the distributor's possession for free, without forcing them to take out a loan to carry them, and then the distributor pays a commission to the parent organization if the products or services sell. Community Enterprise Solutions in Guatemala has used this approach to put thousands of water-purification devices, fuel-efficient stoves, energy-efficient light bulbs, and VisionSpring reading glasses into the hands of the poor, while hundreds of women entrepreneurs have developed sound businesses as distributors.[2]

Branding and Marketing

The business world has recognized the power of brands in today's marketplace. Executives realize that what differentiates one product from another in the vast majority of markets is not its ingredients, style, performance attributes, warranties, or durability. It is the emotional connections that consumers develop with brands that make them feel deeply attached and loyal to their iPhones, Cokes, Nike shoes, Starbucks coffees, or Oakley sunglasses. The nonprofit and social-venture world has recognized the power of brands too, and names like Habitat for Humanity, Teach for America, Race for the Cure, and CityYear have been endowed with special emotional meaning to millions of people, helping these organizations tremendously in fund-raising, attracting volunteers and employees, and lobbying. Recognition of the power of branding is why three reasonably successful social-entrepreneurial organizations have changed their names/brands in the last few years. VisionSpring was originally the ScoJo Foundation, Playworks was originally Sports4Kids, and Fair Trade USA was originally Transfair. In all three cases, the new brands evoke clearer signals about the benefits their organizations are trying to provide to people. They are more likely to pull on the heartstrings of the people they hope to attract for support.

In addition to branding appropriately, replicating requires that serious attention be paid to other aspects of marketing. Much of this involves communicating effectively. But there is more to marketing than branding and communicating. There are the aspects of marketing that involve cultivating distributors and improving customer service to those distributors and end-users. There also may be a need to recruit, train, manage, incentivize, and support a sales force. This will happen when personal communications are essential for implementing your theory of change. An example of an organization that has needed to improve its capabilities with all these other aspects of marketing is the highly publicized Kick Start, which develops new technologies for Africa that are designed to support poverty alleviation. Their best-known product is the Money-Maker irrigation pump that for a low cost can help poor farmers increase their crop yields tremendously—and also potentially earn money from others by leasing out their pump. Kick Start has acknowledged facing substantial challenges in cultivating distributors and forming a sales force. The expense of doing this has meant that large donors/funders often are reluctant to invest in this kind of marketing, not realizing that marketing can be a valuable investment that may not pay dividends immediately, but that can pay off handsomely a few years later.[3]

Replicating around the World: Aflatoun

Jeroo Billimoria's Aflatoun and ChildFinance ventures were discussed earlier as examples of effectiveness in alliance-building.

As mentioned, Billimoria's alliance-building supported her efforts at replicating as well as the building of other organizational capabilities. The approach that Billimoria has employed for replicating deserves more extensive discussion, since I believe she has followed all the advice provided in this current chapter as well as anyone I have seen. The discussion will focus on the replicating done for her Aflatoun program, not for ChildFinance, as the latter venture is built more around a strategy of advocacy (or lobbying) rather than replicating, although the replicating of advocacy approaches in different countries will certainly be considered as ChildFinance progresses.

Aflatoun's mission is to inspire children—especially poor children—"to socially and economically empower themselves to be agents of change in their own lives and for a more equitable world."[4] Aflatoun has developed a program of educational interventions that teach children how to manage money and save, while providing them with greater understanding of social challenges and rights. The curricula are built around activities that involve story-telling, song and dance, games, savings clubs, and financial- and community-improvement enterprises. From its launch in 2005, Aflatoun has grown from operating in 6 countries to operating in 81 by 2011, and it is estimated that they have served over 1.1 million children. The program is delivered through a network of partners that include governments, microfinance institutions, banks, nongovernmental organizations (NGOs), and schools.[5]

Aflatoun has been dedicated from the beginning to understanding what works in teaching children the lessons the organization wants to teach. They have designed their curricula and teaching modules to be consistent with the latest academic research on imparting financial literacy, and they have consulted with experts on this topic on a regular basis. They have also done numerous evaluations of their materials and programs, discovering findings like the following:

• The first Aflatoun pilot in India seemed to increase the children's sense of self-esteem and pride, and to create awareness of the benefits of saving and familiarity with the banking system. Other observed benefits were improved math skills and leadership qualities. And additionally, in an unexpected reversal of the learning model, the parents of children in the program also began to save money.

• The first evaluation of pilot projects outside India was undertaken in May 2007 with a questionnaire to implementing partners. The partners positively evaluated the program and wanted to continue to play a role in implementing and improving it. At the time, 35,000 children participated in the 10 programs outside India, of whom 28,000 were saving money. The Aflatoun organization symbol, a cartoon character of a fireball (popular in Bollywood movies), connected well with children, and the program turned out to be sufficiently versatile to allow for the regional variations required by the implementing partners.[6]

• Pre- and postprogram surveys were done in Nigeria in 2009. From the organization's initial assessment, the program broadened children's conceptions of saving and seemed to increase the likelihood of younger children saving more. Encouragingly, the surveys showed that even within a single Aflatoun year, certain knowledge and attitudes of participants changed. The program's biggest success was in changing perceptions about gender amongst participants. However, child-rights and enterprise indicators did not show significant movement.[7]

Armed with data on what has worked in the past, Aflatoun has created not one, but several curriculum guides and technical assistance guides, to be the "playbooks" that allow scaling to occur more efficiently. These materials have been translated into several languages, and they have been modified in some cases to fit the country context in which they are being used. The main curricula are:

- *Children aged 6–14, formal setting (e.g., schools):* In formal settings, the Aflatoun curriculum is delivered through eight workbooks. These books are available as regional sets in English, French, Spanish, and Arabic. Partners have contextualized their Aflatoun material into 41 editions and 24 different languages.
- *Children and teenagers aged 6–18, nonformal setting:* The *Non-Formal Education* (NFE) *Manual* is designed for the learning facilitators, and can be used for two general target groups: children in need of special protection or nonformal learners (out-of-school youth, street children, abused children in institutions, children in conflict with the law, children in drop-in centers, among others) and children in nonformal settings (microfinance institution clubs, after school clubs). It is designed to address different issues that can make learning challenging for both groups. This book is currently available in six languages: English, Spanish, French, Portuguese, Russian, and Amharic.
- *Teenagers aged 15–18, formal setting:* A curriculum for teenagers (called Aflateen) is designed as a manual for educators and facilitators, and aims to guide young people to reflect on their lives, learn to explore issues and problems in society, and acquire life skills that help them become engaged citizens.

Aflatoun also has created a *Children's Activity Book* that includes a collection of activities and games for teachers or learning facilitators to supplement the other guides.[8]

With high-quality "playbooks," but limited resources for building out branches or satellite offices, the strategy of scaling through affiliation or by franchising became the obvious way to go if Aflatoun was going to have any chance of reaching the millions and millions of poor children who could benefit from the program. The playbooks could help ensure that the program would be taught effectively, but there was also a need for training the staff and volunteers of the affiliates in how to teach the program. Hence, a train-the-trainer model was introduced in which staff of partner organizations went through ten days of training to become Regional Master Trainers, who could then train others. By 2011, Aflatoun had 90 of these Master Trainers.

Aflatoun takes very seriously the determining of affiliates or franchisees, as not all organizations can be trusted to maintain fidelity to the program or to promote the ideas and values that Aflatoun espouses. Affiliates are selected based upon their work with children and their connections within the country, especially with the education system. The affiliates are not compensated for their work, nor do they pay the Aflatoun Secretariat (i.e., home office) a franchise fee for being part of the system. The affiliates must raise their own funds, sometimes by running social enterprises that the children support, in order to keep the program going. Nevertheless, the secretariat supplies considerable technical assistance and support to these partners in developing the required "action plans" and performing other tasks. Moreover, the establishment of a trust relationship, with frequent personal communications using Skype phone calls and other connections, has been a priority, and Billimoria and her staff believe that building trust has been a key to their scaling success. Affiliates become willing to commit great effort to supporting Aflatoun's growth because of the interconnectedness they all feel and the prestige they obtain from being part of this trusting family network.

Aflatoun has paid attention to branding and marketing throughout its scaling efforts, and they have been research-based in how they have made decisions in these areas. For example, the name "Aflatoun" came from discussions with children participating in one of their first programs in India. Aflatoun is a little fireball who comes from outer space, and he appeared in Bollywood movies the children liked.

The organization does marketing to attract franchisees and to draw children to the programs. At first, Aflatoun focused on attracting smaller, more flexible, less risk-averse organizations as franchisees, and then, after they had established more credibility, they targeted larger organizations. In approaching franchisees, Aflatoun has recognized that providing the opportunity for tailoring curricula materials to local conditions is important, and numerous versions of materials have resulted (as discussed above), although the core concepts and philosophy have remained constant across sites. Personal selling and the generation of positive word-of-mouth advertising are important elements of the marketing program. Among the other marketing tools used are:

- a professional website that contains information about the organization's mission and philosophy, curricula materials, the strategic plan, annual reports for all years, evaluation studies, and descriptions of partner organizations;
- a monthly e-newsletter labeled *Aflatoun Talk* that contains updates about new partnerships, growth, research findings, fund-raising accomplishments, and upcoming events;
- an Aflatoun music video designed to help recruit children in Mongolia (see http://www.youtube.com/watch?v=UQYVNx3sRR4). Moreover, there are dozens of other videos available on YouTube that have been used to attract partners or children;

- regular outreach to academics, encouraging them to report on research about Aflatoun at their conferences and in their publications.
- conferences and events for Aflatoun partners are staged all over the world, providing publicity to the organization, opportunities to tell the Aflatoun story to new parties, and chances for partner organizations to network.

These and other tools also serve to generate interest and favorable attitudes toward Aflatoun among the general public and potential donors.

Concluding Comments

Taking your venture to other settings and localities beyond where it achieved its initial success requires developing capabilities at replicating. If your theory of change involves the provision of a product like a "Money-Maker" irrigation pump, and that product can be produced in a way that achieves economies of scale as volumes get larger, then a big part of replicating may come down to being effective at branding and marketing your product. If your theory of change primarily involves the provision of a service or an intervention, like Citizen Schools' after-school program, then replicating requires that you create infrastructure and staff to deliver your program through branches or affiliates, paying attention to maintaining quality control with either approach. Part of this infrastructure often needs to be a "playbook" or guide to help others in new settings implement the program at the same quality level as the original program. Research to support all of this activity, whether it is on what is really working and needs to be replicated, or on what brand name is best, should not be shortchanged. Difficult choices must be made about replicating, and the more information you have to guide your choices, the better.

CHAPTER 9

Stimulating Market Forces: Getting Incentives to Work for You

Every year, I invite a local businessman/entrepreneur to speak to my class in Corporate Social Impact Management. His name is Kevin Trapani, and he is the chief executive officer of The Redwoods Group, a company that has been extremely innovative in generating a strong positive social impact for its clients and their communities. Much of this positive impact can be attributed to Trapani's astute way of aligning several incentives to work for the public good. The Redwoods Group sells liability insurance to YMCAs, Jewish Community Centers, and summer camps. Redwoods makes more money, and their clients are more satisfied, if no one sues or seeks liability compensation from these organizations, eating into Redwoods' reserves. And if no one sues or seeks compensation, then Redwoods can afford to lower their rates and still make good money for their shareholders, pleasing their clients even more and leading them to recommend Redwoods to others. What stimulates all these financial incentives to work are training programs that Redwoods has developed that show their clients how to virtually eliminate drownings and child sexual abuse—the two biggest causes of liability actions against YMCAs, Jewish Community Centers, and camps.

The stimulating market forces organizational capability is defined here as:

> the effectiveness with which the organization creates incentives for people or institutions to engage in market transactions that can help to produce desired social changes.

Though highly related to the earnings-generation capability, the capability of being able to stimulate market forces is different. An organization or its individual fund-raisers may be terrific at generating earnings from private donors, foundations, or governments without using market forces at all. Actually, the ability to harness market forces may allow an organization to cut back on some of its purposeful fundraising efforts, letting the market work its way to providing needed financial resources.

Stimulating market forces also overlaps with communicating, since frequently people need to be persuaded to respond to incentives. Furthermore, overlap with replicating can exist too, as developing an attractive, replicable offering may be needed to stimulate market demand. Indeed, when promoting an innovative product or offering is the basis of an organization's theory of change, the importance of building one's capability in stimulating market forces will intensify. On the other hand, as suggested in the model presented earlier in Figure 3.3, this capability will not be as important to build when the organization already is well endowed with natural resources (and does not have to obtain them on the open market), or when the organization already has access to the markets it wants to operate in and does not need to break down entry barriers.

Successful scaling can certainly be accomplished without an organization being very good at stimulating market forces. However, scaling can happen more rapidly and dramatically when market forces are put to work. For example, the sustainable fishing cause recently got a huge boost when Walmart started to put the Marine Stewardship Council label on all its fish products, indicating that the fish were obtained from sustainable sources and not from waters that were being overfished. The Council created an incentive for Wal-Mart to use the label, persuading the company that their sales of fish would go up if they used the label, since an increasing number of consumers have become concerned about overfishing and would prefer to buy sustainable fish. As other retailers follow Wal-Mart's lead, and more and more consumers buy sustainable fish there and at similar places, additional competitive incentives should come into play and a significant dent should be put in the sales and harvesting of nonsustainable fish.[1]

Stimulating market forces requires you to 1) identify market opportunities, 2) become an active participant in the market, and 3) light a fire under the participants. Each task is discussed below.

Identifying Market Opportunities

There are several different markets that your organization can try to employ in a way that supports your mission. These include:

- financial markets
- philanthropy markets
- labor markets
- business-to-business products/services markets
- consumer products/services markets
- education markets

Financial Markets

Participating in financial markets where debt or equity products are bought and sold is something that can fuel the scaling of certain types of social ventures. Capitalizing on the desires of participants in these markets to make large and growing financial returns can produce positive outcomes for your social cause. For instance, the ability to sell loans that pay profitable interest rates and have high repayment rates has, until recently, fueled the growth of many microfinance organizations, as investors backed these organizations in the hopes of earning strong financial returns. Another example is provided by Self-Help, which was able to expand the number of mortgages it could provide to less-advantaged people because it developed the ability to package groups of mortgages and resell them on the secondary market where investors earned solid returns. Self-Help convinced the Ford Foundation to back these transactions, providing protection to investors against default of these loans. The funds from the investors in the secondary market were then used for additional mortgages.

Engaging "impact investors" is another way to participate in financial markets. There are a growing number of investors who are interested in seeing their investments do well and do good at the same time. Most impact investing will be done with for-profit social ventures, where companies like The Redwoods Group (discussed above) have found ways to make good money and address social problems at the same time. In fact, there is an emerging group of social-venture capital companies like E and Company, Root Capital, and SJF Ventures that help impact investors identify sound investment opportunities, especially in the environmental, health, and housing sectors, where it tends to be more possible to make money and solve social problems simultaneously. Becoming an investment target of one of these social-venture capital companies could be a great way to fuel scaling. To do this, it is necessary to have persuasive (and audited) evidence of financial and social performance.

An organization that is trying to provide evidence of financial and social performance about privately held, smaller companies is B Lab. Indeed, B Lab can be viewed as a social-entrepreneurial organization itself. Their theory of change is basically that providing investors with reliable information about the financial and social performance of companies, will make it easier for organizations to attract investors, which will in turn fuel the growth of the best performers. This information will also lead companies to strive to do better on these measures of performance, creating greater competition on both financial and social dimensions in many industries. B Lab is rating privately held US companies with a system that allows the companies that achieve a reasonably high level of social performance to label themselves as B (for Benefit) Corporations, which can make the companies look good to not only prospective investors but also to consumers, suppliers, and regulatory authorities. The Redwoods Group is a B Corporation. The B Corp ratings are created using a self-administered online questionnaire, with B Lab staff members checking the answers for accuracy during visits to the company. B Lab is also using a similar online questionnaire to create ratings of social venture capital firms and international for-profit, socially oriented businesses. They are calling this international rating system GIIRS—the Global Impact Investing Rating System—and the answers to these questions are to be reviewed by a major international public accounting firm in the hopes of generating investor confidence in the metrics.[2]

However, if you are a nonprofit social venture, opportunities for participation in financial markets may be more limited. There is interest recently in the concept of "social impact bonds," and that mechanism may become an option for some nonprofits. The way this works is that a lender buys a bond that provides funds for the nonprofit to pursue a program that has the promise of alleviating a financially costly social problem—think of problems like prison recidivism, obesity, or dementia. If the nonprofit is successful at achieving certain benchmark metrics that demonstrate that money has been saved, a government agency or insurance company that saved money because of the program pays back the lender, adding a nice extra financial return to the payoff. If the benchmark metrics are not met, then the government agency or insurance company would be off the hook for a payback, and the lender would treat the loan as a charitable deduction. Thus far, these bonds have been experimented with in England for a program designed to reduce prison recidivism, but one can envision more widespread use of this idea once a variety of legal matters are settled about how to treat such bonds.[3]

A similar concept to the social impact bonds is the Lumni "human capital investment," which is being used in Columbia to finance college educations for poor students. To date, 1,900 students have received financing of varying amounts. When they accept this money, the students enter into a contract to pay a certain percentage of their earnings for a certain number of years to the investor (all of this is negotiated in advance). The idea is to give investors a sound return on their money, while also putting the students in a situation where they are not saddled with a fixed amount of debt that is piling up huge interest payments. Instead, the students pay a reasonable and affordable percentage of their salaries for a period of time.

The better the students do in the salary department, the better the returns to the investors.[4]

Philanthropy Markets

While conventional financial markets may not be available to nonprofit social ventures—and social impact bonds may not become a reality until years from now—nonprofits definitely have the potential to obtain "investments" from philanthropists and foundations. As stressed over and over again in this book, you still need to demonstrate clear social-impact results to these philanthropists, as well as an ability to become at least partially financially sustainable on your own, but you don't have to show an ability to make a financial return for the philanthropist. However, it helps to recognize that philanthropists/foundations tend to compete with one another for bragging rights to say they have had more social impact than another philanthropy/foundation.

An interesting strategy for stimulating interest in the philanthropy market is for an organization to win awards. Starting with winning a small social-entrepreneurial business-plan competition or something similar at a university event or a conference, it may be possible for an organization to move from that to becoming an Ashoka fellow or Echoing Green awardee—wonderful credentials with which relatively young social-entrepreneurial ventures can brand themselves. And awards for early-stage ventures can often lead to awards or funding from other philanthropists, such as the Skoll Foundation, the Schwab Foundation, and the Draper-Richards Foundation. All have developed a set of awardees or fellows that they fund for multiple years and publicize heavily. Interestingly, several people we have talked about in this book—like John Mighton of JUMP Math, Jeroo Billimoria of ChildFinance, Jordan

Kassalow of VisionSpring, Eric Schwarz of Citizen Schools, and Paul Rice of Fair Trade USA—have become awardees or fellows of more than one foundation. Frankly, philanthropists like to avoid making mistakes, so they are prone to adopt a nonrisky strategy like funding organizations or individuals that have already received recognition from others.

Labor Markets

Several social ventures have been helped tremendously in their scaling by their ability to get what they want from labor markets. Teach for America taps into the labor market of recent college graduates, having become a prestigious and selective place for those graduates to spend their first two years after graduation. Girls on the Run has done very well tapping the volunteer labor market, attracting numerous young women or young parents to be coaches, fund-raisers, or administrative support.

Business-to-Business Products/Services Markets

Scaling has been supported in some cases by a social venture creating and marketing a high-value product or service that purchasing agents and other organizational buyers view as performing better per dollar spent than the competition. An organization's promoting offerings that buyers view as saving them money, or as helping their organizations make more money, attracts buyers. Many social ventures have thus benefited from developing catering services, office moving services, and so on. For example, the organization mentioned in chapter 7, Specialist People, employs autistic persons who are better at testing software than others, thus providing great value to its clients. And REDF, discussed at the end of that same chapter, provides technical assistance to numerous nonprofits that make good money from business-to-business services like trash removal, landscape maintenance, and building management.

Consumer Products/Services Markets

Similar to the case for business-to-business markets, consumer markets will respond to high-value offerings. Several social ventures have scaled more successfully because they have come up with products/services for which consumers are clamoring. Fair-trade coffee and chocolate come to mind (see below), as does sustainable seafood. Another example is provided by the organization Elvis and Kresse, which recycles old fire hoses from the United Kingdom and converts them into very fashionable high-end handbags, attaché cases, and so forth that people are proud to purchase, in part because 50 percent of the profits on these items are donated to the Fire Fighters Charity. The group has also arranged endorsements from celebrities like Cameron Diaz, which has also helped to create consumer appeal.[5]

Education Markets

Charter schools and private schools with unique curricula, teachers, and facilities—as well as good word-of-mouth from parents—have often had more success than their counterparts in the education market. Understanding how to operate in this market has helped organizations like Playworks, Citizens Schools, and Harlem Children's Zone in their scaling efforts.

Becoming a Player

It is one thing to identify an opportunity to help your scaling by becoming a participant in a functioning market, while it is quite another to become a "player" in that market. Barriers to entry exist in many markets that may prevent your participation. Entrenched players in some markets may have brand loyalties or deals with suppliers or distributors that may block you. Or these entrenched players may be poised to under-price or out-advertise your efforts to succeed in attracting businesses or consumers to your social enterprise. Knowing how to promote and market your offering in a competitively sustainable way is essential, as operations like Divine Chocolate, which sells fair-trade products through Whole Foods and, also, through more conventional supermarkets, have clearly learned (see more on fair trade below).

In addition, legal or licensing requirements may make it difficult to operate in some markets, including some financial, labor, or education markets. It may take successful legal maneuvering and/or lobbying to gain access to some markets. Recall the example of Benetech in chapter 6, which had so much difficulty navigating the political issues in trying to break into the market for land-mine-detection equipment that it gave up on the initiative. On the other hand, as discussed above, Self-Help was able to break into the mortgage secondary market, relying heavily on the backing it received from the Ford Foundation to pave its way.

Lighting a Fire

As suggested, part of becoming a player may have to do with being good at promoting and marketing an offering. It may be important to motivate people to buy your offering or, if you are seeking behavior changes like preventive health actions, motivate people to be less self-destructive and more socially responsible.

Clearly, creating a "buzz" about what your organization is trying to achieve will help incentivize behavior and stimulate market participants to engage in desired types of transactions. Think about how much Teach for America has benefited from the buzz it has created among college students about what a great option it is for recent graduates. Similarly, organizations like Harlem Children's Zone, Knowledge Is Power Program (KIPP) Schools, City Year, YouthBuild, and Habitat for Humanity have reaped rewards from their ability to create lots of positive word-of-mouth and excitement about their programs.

Stimulating Multiple Markets Simultaneously: Fair Trade USA

Earlier in the book, I provided an image of a theory of change or logic model for using the creation and promotion of a fair-trade chocolate program as a mechanism for improving the lives of cacao growers in developing countries, as well as for preserving the natural environment in which they live. The idea here is to encourage labor markets and consumer markets—supported by financial and philanthropy markets—to operate in ways that provide improved returns for plantation owners, better working conditions and pay for workers, great products for consumers, and strong returns for the distributors and retailers that serve those consumers, and that cause less harm to the environment where the cacao is grown. Setting up a trustworthy certification system with inspections, along with consultation about how to operate in a "fair" manner, are essential to make this system work. With astute orchestration, a fair-trade program can scale its social impact rapidly, since the financial incentives in the system can motivate behavior in ways that may not exist for other types of scaling efforts.

   An organization that seems to be mastering the orchestration of fair-trade systems is Fair Trade USA, started by Paul

Rice in 1998 (under the name of Transfair).[6] Rice had previously spent 11 years working as a rural development specialist, primarily in Latin America, and he learned about fair trade while leading an organic coffee export cooperative. Over the last 13 years, Fair Trade USA has made a difference in the lives of coffee growers around the world, and they are beginning to produce similar impacts with growers of cacao, bananas, vegetables, flowers, nuts, and herbs. They are also promoting fair-trade apparel, wine, body-care products, and sports balls.

Fair Trade USA recognizes that they need to stimulate demand simultaneously on both ends of the supply chain. They have to encourage growers/manufacturers and their workers to be excited about and committed to operating by certain standards, while also attracting consumers and their retailers to be clamoring for fair-trade products—and even be willing to pay a premium for them over competing products. They have found this to be easier to do in some markets than others, but they are making significant progress in most. The organization's latest promotional materials claim that there are now 9,500 Fair Trade USA products sold in 60,000 US retail locations, generating $1.2 billion in retail sales and benefiting 1.2 million farmers and workers with $56 million in community-development funds. Further, their studies show that 34 percent of US consumers are now aware of the Fair Trade Certified label, and that 87 percent of them indicate that they trust what the label says.

The team at Fair Trade USA has been reasonably systematic about identifying market opportunities. They tend to focus first on supplier and labor markets, looking for situations where they feel confident that they can certify that fair labor practices are being employed, living wages are being paid, and environmental protection is being pursued. They also want to be able to help suppliers with financing, and have worked with financial institutions to facilitate the provision of microcredit. With Rice's background with coffee, and with a longer history of fair-trade coffee certification receiving a following in Europe, it was natural to be most aggressive in trying to expand the fair-trade coffee market first. Working with growers and cooperatives in developing countries like Nicaragua and Brazil, Fair Trade USA has become confident that they can guide them toward supplying excellent quality beans while at the same time employing fair-trade practices, and these experiences have provided stories and a degree of evidence that has proven persuasive to "partners" that fill the supply chain for coffee. Hundreds of importers, roasters, manufacturers, and retailers of coffee, including well-known brands like Starbucks and Peet's, have become licensed partners with Fair Trade USA. These licensees are also persuaded to become part of this system by research that Fair Trade USA has accumulated that found that 18 percent of the US population are "advocates" for fair trade and are willing to spend up to 5 percent more for certified products. The research also suggests that as many as 31 percent more are "ready to join" the "advocates." These data are helpful in recruiting the larger partners that put more emphasis on financial numbers than the emotional story of fair trade. The licensing fees paid by these partners, which give them the right to claim that they are selling Fair Trade Certified products, have contributed to Fair Trade USA being able to cover 75 percent of its budget with earned-income revenues.

The philanthropy market is where Fair Trade USA attempts to cover the remaining part of its budget. Rice and his colleagues have been very active in fund-raising and have won numerous grants and awards. Stories and metrics are essential in the philanthropy market too, and Rice and his partners have become very effective at using them to make their case.

But reliance on the philanthropy market is risky, so cultivating the "advocates" and "ready to joins" in the consumer market is essential to keep the revenue flowing from the partners and expanding their numbers. There is still considerable untapped demand in the US market for fair-trade coffee, and they have only scratched the surface on the market potential for other fair-trade products. Hence, Fair Trade USA is trying hard to promote the fair-trade cause with publicity and advocacy. They have also produced an advertising campaign with the headline of "every cup matters" (often substituting the word "spoonful" or "touch" for the word "cup") that has appeared on websites like epicurious.com, on billboards and transit advertising, and through social media like Facebook.

One of the opportunities that can be capitalized upon with this campaign and other advocacy efforts is how people are feeling recently about "organics" and "natural" foods. Many people are developing a skepticism about these labels, since a widely trusted certification or labeling system has not emerged for them, and consumers are not really sure they are buying healthier and environmentally friendlier products just because a sign in the produce department says "organic" or "natural." Fair Trade USA is hoping that its certification system and label will win over consumers who have this skepticism about organics and natural labels to the broad range of products with the Fair Trade label. Regardless, becoming a "player" in the supply chain for vegetables, fruits, and chocolate is a whole different ballgame than what the organization has experienced with coffee, and Fair Trade USA certainly faces many challenges in pursing these opportunities. Yet their website is filled with reports on how much impact they have had in supply chains like the one for bananas.

Another approach to cultivating consumer demand and accomplishing the "lighting a fire" discussed in this chapter is by promoting the development of Fair Trade Towns and Fair Trade Universities. Funded by external donors, the campaign to build these communities has already recruited towns like Healdsburg, California; Brattleboro, Vermont; Milwaukee, Wisconsin; Amherst, Massachusetts; Taos, New Mexico; Northampton, Massachusetts; San Francisco, California; Montclair, New Jersey; Ballston Spa, New York; Chico, California; and Bluffton, Ohio. The University of Wisconsin Oshkosh became the first university to sign on to this effort. The approach of these initiatives is articulated as follows:

> Fair Trade Towns unites conscious consumers, dedicated activists, members of the business and retail community, local communities of faith and other community organizations, and your city or town government in the effort to ensure that we are all playing a part in supporting those who provide us with so much in the US market. Through dynamic events, meetings, online organizing and other outreach we bring together a diverse group of community members to expand the message of the importance of Fair Trade and unite our communities behind a banner of global justice and equity.

They have had considerable success in convincing the governments, schools, nonprofits, businesses, and other institutions in these communities to commit to upholding fair-trade principles and to purchase fair-trade products whenever possible.

With their efforts to transform whole communities, Fair Trade USA is attempting to orchestrate the kind of ecosystem change discussed at the end of chapter 1. They realize that their efforts to scale social impact can become more fruitful if they can turn fair trade from a cause supported by a significant and passionate minority into a cause that has a whole social movement behind it. If they can get consumers clamoring for fair-trade products of all types—and not just coffee—and get retailers, campuses, government agencies, and institutions to change policies and procedures to encourage the purchase and merchandising of fair-trade products, then the benefits could redound to people all over the world involved with the creation and manufacture of those products.

Concluding Comments

Letting market forces carry you to greater scaling success is an admirable goal, and several social ventures have found a way to make this happen. When financiers, philanthropists, employee prospects, volunteer prospects, businesses, consumers, and students are demanding and competing for your patronage or offerings, then funding can be generated and other favorable outcomes can occur. The ideal situation is one that is a win-win, such as the one identified by Trapani and his insurance company, The Redwoods Group, which makes more money the more it can prevent drownings and child sexual abuse. Seeking these "sweet spots" where incentives align for multiple parties can produce significant social impacts.

CHAPTER 10

Putting It All Together: Embracing Contingencies and Complexity

B uilding up all of the SCALERS capabilities in the ways described in this book can be a daunting challenge. In this last chapter, I would like to lead you through a step-by-step approach for finalizing a scaling strategy that fits your ecosystem situation and has a reasonable chance for success. The approach involves your answering a set of questions as carefully and honestly as possible, and, depending on the answers, choosing from among a more limited set of pathways to scale. These questions should provide a vehicle for you to obtain a better sense for whether the relationships proposed in Figure 3.3 actually work in your situation. The questions steer you through an assessment of (1) your scaling success to date, (2) your theory of change, (3) your starting resources, and (4) your organizational capabilities. Many of the questions originated from previous empirical research that my colleagues and I have done on the determinants of successful scaling.[1]

The questions have been designed so that a well-informed manager from virtually any type of social-entrepreneurial organization can answer them. They are not designed only for organizations working in certain sectors or problem areas, such as education or poverty alleviation. Admittedly, there is a chance that by the questions being so generic, they may miss some nuances of what is happening in an organization. Readers should therefore feel free to edit and expand on the questions presented here to create a self-assessment instrument that is tailored to the situation and demands of their own organization.

Self-Assessment of Scaling Success

A starting point is to ask the following questions about how well your organization is doing at the present time in scaling social impact. If after completing these questions you realize that you are already doing all you will ever be capable of doing to address a given social problem, then scaling should not be a goal, and you should probably focus on other issues (e.g., cost control) besides building the SCALERS capabilities. On the other hand, if these questions lead you to believe that you have much to accomplish in scaling, then the answers from your first completion of this questionnaire can serve as very useful baseline measures of scaling success at a given time, which can then be used as comparison points at some future time to determine whether you have made significant progress in scaling.

Start by thinking about your organization relative to other similar ones and answer as best you can.

Compared to other organizations working to resolve similar social problems as your organization . . .

1. . . . we are satisfied with how much we have alleviated the problem.

Strongly Disagree   **Strongly Agree**
      1   2   3   4   5   6   7

2. ...we have scaled up our capabilities to address the problem.

Strongly Disagree   Strongly Agree

    1   2   3   4   5   6   7

3. ...we are in better shape than anyone else to have an impact on the problem.

Strongly Disagree   Strongly Agree

    1   2   3   4   5   6   7

4. ...we are less frustrated with the progress we are making on the problem.

Strongly Disagree   Strongly Agree

    1   2   3   4   5   6   7

5. ...we are getting a better *social* return on our investment.

Strongly Disagree   Strongly Agree

    1   2   3   4   5   6   7

6. ...we have had a better ratio of successes to failures with our initiatives.

Strongly Disagree   Strongly Agree

    1   2   3   4   5   6   7

An average score of around 6 or more on these six items would suggest that there is not much to accomplish with scaling this organization—at least compared to other organizations with similar missions. Of course, this could be a consequence of there being comparable organizations that are scaling very poorly, not that the organization is doing so well. It is important to examine which explanation is more valid. If it turns out the organization is indeed doing very well at scaling, then attention to matters like controlling costs could make sense. However, it is more likely that your organization will receive an average score of much less than six, indicating that there is lots of room for improving scaling results. For one thing, you probably wouldn't be reading this book if you didn't feel a need to scale.

In addition to the scores on these six items, there are other numbers you can examine to help you assess how well you are doing at scaling at the present time. The size of your budget, your number of employees, your number of volunteers, and your number of people served can all be indicators of how well you are doing at scaling. You might also consider less directly related measures reflecting the extent of a social problem, such as the number of deaths caused by a certain disease or the number of days of poor air quality in a region. Monitoring how any metrics of scaling success change from time period to time period—and seeing whether these change scores move in the same direction as the change in the SCALERS scores (covered below) and in proportionally greater or lesser magnitude than the SCALERS scores—can be very instructive for refining your scaling strategy.

Self-Assessment of Theory of Change

The following set of questions should allow you to hone in on what the emphasis seems to be in your theory of change.

To what extent would you say your organization is relying on each of the approaches listed below to help it scale its social impact? Please answer from Very Little to Very Much on the seven-point scales.

1. **Using lots of talented people to provide services**

Very Little   **Very Much**

   1   2   3   4   5   6   7

2. Disseminating and publicizing ideas about new ways of approaching a social problem

Very Little   Very Much

     1   2   3   4   5   6   7

3. Collaborating with other organizations with complementary interests

Very Little   Very Much

     1   2   3   4   5   6   7

4. Obtaining a change in public policy (i.e., a law, regulation, or budgetary allocation)

Very Little   Very Much

     1   2   3   4   5   6   7

5. Providing financial capital to social-purpose organizations

Very Little   Very Much

     1   2   3   4   5   6   7

6. Using technology to help match people or organizations with similar needs or to create more efficiency in logistics

Very Little   Very Much

     1   2   3   4   5   6   7

7. Obtaining adoption and use of an innovative new product or process

Very Little   Very Much

     1   2   3   4   5   6   7

The higher the score you provide on any of these seven items, the more important certain SCALERS are likely to be in driving social impact for your organization. Figure 3.3 shows how the different theory bases line up with different SCALERS. To sum up, the figure shows that

- greater reliance on labor-intensive interventions should make it more important for staffing to be strong;
- greater reliance on dissemination of ideas and information should make it more important for communicating to be strong;
- greater reliance on collaboration should make it more important for alliance-building to be strong;
- greater reliance on public-policy change should make it more important for lobbying to be strong;
- greater reliance on financial stimulus should make it more important for earnings-generation to be strong;
- greater reliance on matching and logistics should make it more important for replicating to be strong;
- greater reliance on an innovative product or service should make it more important for stimulating market forces to be strong.

Most organizations are likely to score high on one of these seven items, but not on the others, as few social ventures try to implement multiple types of interventions at once. So depending on how you answer these seven questions, you may be able to achieve some focus in your scaling efforts, putting more emphasis on building a single SCALER capability than the others. That does not mean that you can forget about all the other SCALERS, as all the capabilities will probably need to be there at a sufficient level for scaling to happen. Moreover, depending on your starting resources, which you will assess next, certain other SCALERS may become elevated in importance.

Self-Assessment of Starting Resources

If your examination of your ecosystem indicates that you have a deficit of key resources when either starting a brand new scaling effort or renewing a scaling effort after initial successes have been consolidated, then you must place major emphasis in your scaling strategy on building capabilities that tend to support the accumulation of those resources that are lacking. The following set of questions can be used to assess your present resource situation. The questions are phrased to get you to think about your situation today, not what it was in the past. The idea here is for readers to go through the questions to determine a strategy for the future, no matter what point they are leaping off from.

The questions about starting resources are organized around the different types of capital that have been discussed throughout the book. All of the resource categories are assessed based on three questions each, with the exception of social capital, which is assessed with six questions—reflecting a desire to tap into how the organization is doing with individuals (three items) and potential allied organizations (three items).

As was the case with the scaling success questions, think about your organization relative to other similar ones and answer as best you can.

Compared to other organizations working to resolve similar social problems as your organization...

A. Human Capital

1. ...we have people in place who possess the skills necessary to run our programs.

Strongly Disagree   Strongly Agree
    1   2   3   4   5   6   7

2. ...we have individuals in management positions with the skills necessary to lead our organization.

Strongly Disagree   Strongly Agree
       1   2   3   4   5   6   7

3. ...we have individuals on our board with the skills necessary to guide our organization.

Strongly Disagree   Strongly Agree
       1   2   3   4   5   6   7

B. Social Capital

1. ...we are not pursuing a very controversial cause.

Strongly Disagree   Strongly Agree
       1   2   3   4   5   6   7

2. ...we find people really love what we are doing.

Strongly Disagree   Strongly Agree
       1   2   3   4   5   6   7

3. ...we rarely step on anyone's toes in pursuing our initiatives.

Strongly Disagree   Strongly Agree
       1   2   3   4   5   6   7

4. ...we find many other organizations interested in our cause.

Strongly Disagree   Strongly Agree
       1   2   3   4   5   6   7

5. ...we do not have anything about us that creates barriers to attracting ally organizations.

Strongly Disagree   Strongly Agree
       1   2   3   4   5   6   7

6. ...we are not alone as an organization that is concerned with our cause.

Strongly Disagree   Strongly Agree

  1   2   3   4   5   6   7

C. Political Capital

1. ...we have very few laws or regulations that make it difficult for us to pursue our mission.

Strongly Disagree   Strongly Agree

  1   2   3   4   5   6   7

2. ...we do not find governments or public policy getting in the way of what we want to do.

Strongly Disagree   Strongly Agree

  1   2   3   4   5   6   7

3. ...we never face a political climate that is averse to our cause.

Strongly Disagree   Strongly Agree

  1   2   3   4   5   6   7

D. Financial Capital

1. ...we have plenty of funding to do what we want to do.

Strongly Disagree   Strongly Agree

  1   2   3   4   5   6   7

2. ...we have a sufficient supply of financial capital.

Strongly Disagree   Strongly Agree

  1   2   3   4   5   6   7

3. ...we are not just scraping by financially.

Strongly Disagree   Strongly Agree

  1   2   3   4   5   6   7

E. Technological Capital

1. ...we have access to the telecommunications equipment we need.

Strongly Disagree   Strongly Agree

1   2   3   4   5   6   7

2. ...we have access to the computer and information technology we need.

Strongly Disagree   Strongly Agree

1   2   3   4   5   6   7

3. ...we have smoothly functioning and efficient systems for logistics and transportation, and for conducting our operations.

Strongly Disagree   Strongly Agree

1   2   3   4   5   6   7

F. Natural-Resource Capital

1. ...we have no trouble obtaining any of the raw materials or supplies we need to deliver our products or programs.

Strongly Disagree   Strongly Agree

1   2   3   4   5   6   7

2. ... we are not endangering any natural resources in the way we are delivering our programs.

Strongly Disagree   Strongly Agree

1   2   3   4   5   6   7

3. ...we do not have a serious problem finding sources of supply for products we need to use or sell.

Strongly Disagree   Strongly Agree

1   2   3   4   5   6   7

G. Access to Markets

1. ...we have no trouble gaining access to places where we can sell the things we want to sell.

Strongly Disagree   Strongly Agree
     1   2   3   4   5   6   7

2. ... the best places to sell our offerings are easily available to us.

Strongly Disagree   Strongly Agree
     1   2   3   4   5   6   7

3. ... we do not face strong competitors in the markets we are trying to serve.

Strongly Disagree   Strongly Agree
     1   2   3   4   5   6   7

Average scores of 6 or more for the questions in any of these resource categories would imply that the organization is well endowed in that category and may not need to emphasize the building of the corresponding capability in the immediate future. This means that

- a high score on human capital may reduce the importance of building the staffing capability;
- a high score on social capital may reduce the importance of building the communicating capability;
- a high score on social capital may reduce the importance of building the alliance-building capability;
- a high score on political capital may reduce the importance of building the lobbying capability;
- a high score on financial capital may reduce the importance of building the earnings-generation capability;

- a high score on technological capital may reduce the importance of building the replicating capability;
- a high score on natural-resource capital may reduce the importance of building the stimulating market forces capability;
- a high score on access to markets may reduce the importance of building the stimulating market forces capability.

Again, depending on how you answer the starting-resource questions, you may be able to achieve some focus in your scaling efforts, putting more emphasis on building a few SCALERS capabilities where you are starting out with weakness in comparison with the others.

Self-Assessment of Organizational Capabilities

The questions about starting resources are meant to tap how you feel about the *assets* you already have in your possession as you commence or renew your scaling efforts. This next set of questions is designed to mine how you feel about your level of competence in creating processes and procedures that are able to build or accumulate those assets. The assets and competences will tend to be correlated, as exhibiting competence at something like communicating should demonstrate itself in higher levels of social capital, while low competence in communicating would reveal low social capital. But such correlations do not always have to exist. For example, one can imagine a situation where an organization might actually be starting out weak on something like financial capital but have a strong business model, with plenty of earnings-generation capabilities, that will rather quickly transform its financial capital into a strong asset.

The seven SCALERS capabilities categories are each assessed using five questions, with the exception of staffing, which is tapped with eight questions, and replicating, which is tapped with six questions. As was the case with the scaling-success and starting-resources questions, think about your organization relative to other similar ones and answer as best you can.

Thinking about the recent operations of your entire organization, please indicate how strongly you agree or disagree with each of the following statements, assuming each statement starts with the following phrase:

Compared to other organizations working to resolve similar social problems as your organization...

A. Staffing (Human Resources Capabilities)

1. ...we have little difficulty filling all our labor needs with competent people.

Strongly Disagree   Strongly Agree

1   2   3   4   5   6   7

2. ...we have been effective at meeting our labor needs with people who have the necessary skills.

Strongly Disagree   Strongly Agree

1   2   3   4   5   6   7

3. ...we have an ample pool of capable volunteers available to help us meet our labor needs.

Strongly Disagree   Strongly Agree

1   2   3   4   5   6   7

4. ...we are effective at recruiting and retaining people for important paid staff positions.

Strongly Disagree   Strongly Agree

1   2   3   4   5   6   7

5. ...we do not face a problem with a talent shortage.

Strongly Disagree   Strongly Agree
    1   2   3   4   5   6   7

6. ...we have been able to attract appropriate and helpful people to our board.

Strongly Disagree   Strongly Agree
    1   2   3   4   5   6   7

7. ...we have developed an efficient, smoothly functioning organizational structure.

Strongly Disagree   Strongly Agree
    1   2   3   4   5   6   7

8. ...we have taken strategic planning seriously.

Strongly Disagree   Strongly Agree
    1   2   3   4   5   6   7

B. Communicating

1. ...we have been effective at communicating what we do to key constituencies and stakeholders.

Strongly Disagree   Strongly Agree
    1   2   3   4   5   6   7

2. ...we have done a good job of getting "our story" out to the public.

Strongly Disagree   Strongly Agree
    1   2   3   4   5   6   7

3. ...we have been successful at informing the people we seek to serve about the benefits and costs of what we can do for them.

Strongly Disagree   Strongly Agree
    1   2   3   4   5   6   7

4. ...we have been successful at informing donors and funders about the value of what we do.

Strongly Disagree   Strongly Agree

1   2   3   4   5   6   7

5. ...we have been successful at persuading individuals to change their own personal behaviors to help alleviate the social problem we address.

Strongly Disagree   Strongly Agree

1   2   3   4   5   6   7

C. Alliance-building

1. ...we have built partnerships with other organizations that have been win-win situations for us and them.

Strongly Disagree   Strongly Agree

1   2   3   4   5   6   7

2. ...we rarely try to "go it alone" when pursuing new initiatives.

Strongly Disagree   Strongly Agree

1   2   3   4   5   6   7

3. ...we have accomplished more through joint action with other organizations than we could have by flying solo.

Strongly Disagree   Strongly Agree

1   2   3   4   5   6   7

4. ...we do not worry about "owning" an issue and are willing to share credit with others for any successes.

Strongly Disagree   Strongly Agree

1   2   3   4   5   6   7

5. ...we take advantage of synergies between our organization and other organizations.

Strongly Disagree   Strongly Agree
   1   2   3   4   5   6   7

D. Lobbying

1. ...we have been successful at getting government agencies and officials to provide financial support for our efforts.

Strongly Disagree   Strongly Agree
   1   2   3   4   5   6   7

2. ...we have been successful at getting government agencies and officials to create laws, rules, and regulations that support our efforts.

Strongly Disagree   Strongly Agree
   1   2   3   4   5   6   7

3. ...we have been able to raise our cause to a higher place on the public agenda.

Strongly Disagree   Strongly Agree
   1   2   3   4   5   6   7

4. ...we have increased the amount of public discourse about our cause.

Strongly Disagree   Strongly Agree
   1   2   3   4   5   6   7

5. ...we rarely have difficulty getting political figures to consider our arguments.

Strongly Disagree   Strongly Agree
   1   2   3   4   5   6   7

E. Earnings Generation

1. ...we have generated a strong stream of revenues from products and services that we sell for a price.

Strongly Disagree   Strongly Agree

   1   2   3   4   5   6   7

2. ...we have donors and funders who have been generous with us.

Strongly Disagree   Strongly Agree

   1   2   3   4   5   6   7

3. ...we do not feel pressure to find new sources of revenue.

Strongly Disagree   Strongly Agree

   1   2   3   4   5   6   7

4. ...we have had little trouble paying our bills.

Strongly Disagree   Strongly Agree

   1   2   3   4   5   6   7

5. ...we have found ways to finance our activities that keep us sustainable.

Strongly Disagree   Strongly Agree

   1   2   3   4   5   6   7

F. Replicating

1. ...we have a "package" or "system" that can work effectively in multiple locations or situations.

Strongly Disagree   Strongly Agree

   1   2   3   4   5   6   7

2. ...we do not face a highly unique situation in every place we operate.

Strongly Disagree   Strongly Agree

1   2   3   4   5   6   7

3. ...we find it easy to replicate our programs.

Strongly Disagree   Strongly Agree

1   2   3   4   5   6   7

4. ...we have little difficulty teaching new branches or affiliates what we do.

Strongly Disagree   Strongly Agree

1   2   3   4   5   6   7

5. ...we do not incur large expenses when replicating our programs.

Strongly Disagree   Strongly Agree

1   2   3   4   5   6   7

6. ...we have conducted evaluations that provide evidence that our programs are worth replicating.

Strongly Disagree   Strongly Agree

1   2   3   4   5   6   7

G. Stimulating Market Forces

1. ...we have been able to demonstrate that businesses can make money through supporting our initiatives.

Strongly Disagree   Strongly Agree

1   2   3   4   5   6   7

2. ...we have been able to demonstrate that consumers/organizations can save money through patronizing our products and services.

Strongly Disagree   Strongly Agree

1   2   3   4   5   6   7

3. ...we have created incentives (i.e., financial rewards, recognition) that resonate with investors, consumers, and others.

Strongly Disagree   Strongly Agree

1   2   3   4   5   6   7

4. ...we have found the pursuit of self-interest by businesses and consumers has led to good outcomes for our cause.

Strongly Disagree   Strongly Agree

1   2   3   4   5   6   7

5. ...we have been able to trust market forces to help resolve social problems.

Strongly Disagree   Strongly Agree

1   2   3   4   5   6   7

Average scores of 3 or below for any of the SCALERS capabilities would indicate a real weakness in that area. Such scores may represent a very important challenge for the organization if the answers to the theory-of-change and starting-resource questions point to that SCALERS capability as one that is especially important for scaling success. Of course, the material in chapters 3 through 9 provides ideas on how to build up each of the SCALERS capabilities.

Putting It All Together

Doing a conscientious job of answering questions like those posed in this chapter should be helpful to you, but remember that these questions were designed to be generic. Clearly, more detailed questions about theories of change, starting resources, and the SCALERS capabilities could be designed and, while such a tailored instrument may make it hard to compare data across organizations at a given point in time, it could be very useful, as discussed previously, for tracking an organization's capabilities and accomplishments over time.

Let me offer an example of how an organization might use the questions in this chapter. Assume that a social service agency in a large city has developed an innovative credit-counseling class that it delivers in a single, three-hour session to people that have gotten in over their head with credit. Let's say this class has been the subject of an evaluation, which found that when participants were surveyed two months after taking the class, they reported better scores on measures of their financial-planning practices, reductions in their use of credit, and improvements in their credit scores—as compared to what they reported before they took the class and compared to a "hold-out" group (randomly assigned) that had not yet had the chance to take the class. So it appears that the agency has a program that "works" and could really help people, especially if it could be scaled up.

Assume that after having a team of managers, as well as an outside volunteer consultant, complete the questions in this chapter as well as a few supplemental questions provided by the consultant, the mean scores on each question (and for each section) lead the team to conclude that

- the agency has managed to run classes for several years at a few sites, but it has not really scaled up to have a significant social impact on credit-stretched consumers in the agency's local area, its region, or the entire country;

- the basic theory of change that they are pursuing involves the dissemination of ideas and information (in a nicely designed class) to credit-stretched consumers. There is some reliance on collaborations with financial institutions, libraries, community colleges, and other social service agencies to help spread the word about and provide venues for the classes, but other theories of change, such as using a labor-intensive intervention, are not really in play here. Indeed, the idea is to use the classes as an efficient intervention that replaces the one-on-one counseling traditionally done by the agency;
- the starting resources for a scaling effort are barely adequate for the organization, with a little more strength in human capital (a stable of dedicated credit counselors), political capital (supportive city officials and state legislators), and technological capital (sound email and database system), but with weakness in social capital (not very well known or appreciated) and financial capital (just scraping by);
- given the emphases of its theory of change and its starting resources, the organization needs to focus on communicating, alliance-building, and earnings-generation as areas to improve its capabilities. The fact that the managers and consultant gave the organization low scores on these three capabilities reinforces the need to focus on them.

Building its capabilities in these three areas will be challenging, and the organization should seek opportunities to obtain synergies in the building of these capabilities. Aggressive pursuit of a major corporation as a sponsor/partner is worth a serious try. Perhaps a financial institution like a major bank or credit union would find it advantageous to have its brand associated with these classes and actually host some of them at its facilities. The institution could publicize the classes in advertising and in the signage in its branches, and it could even have tellers and other personnel talk up the opportunity (and perhaps teach the classes). Maybe a small licensing fee could be paid to the social-service agency every time the financial institution uses the class material. Hopefully, a financial institution would feel an incentive to support this program, even though, if its customers start to manage their money more wisely, the institution would lose late fees, interest payments, and other sources of revenue. Presumably, these losses could be compensated for by the institution having fewer foreclosures and bankruptcies to deal with, as well as by having more customers that switch to this institution in appreciation of its consumer-friendly programs.

Unfortunately, most organizations will not find it as easy as this social service agency to converge on a scaling strategy. For most organizations that are just starting a scaling effort, it will be very difficult to answer all the questions accurately and obtain a clear picture of the implications of the answers for formulating a strategic direction. The real world of scaling is extremely complicated and challenging. Even if the organization has had some success with scaling and is using the questions and SCALERS framework to reassess what it has accomplished and where it should go next, complications and challenges will emerge.

Nevertheless, I feel confident that making a serious attempt to follow the advice in this chapter will put your organization in a better position for scaling its impact than it might be otherwise.

Concluding Comments

Using the SCALERS framework and the ideas in this book in a manner similar to this last social-service agency example seems highly feasible for many organizations. Scaling is actually incredibly difficult, and that is why so few organizations can be identified as scaling success stories. Regardless, following a systematic approach of asking and answering questions like those posed in this chapter should improve your chances for scaling success.

Notes

Preface

1. Chip Heath and Dan Heath, *Made to Stick* (New York: Random House) (2007).
2. Paul N. Bloom and Aaron K. Chatterji, "Scaling Social Entrepreneurial Impact," California Management Review (Spring 2009), 114–133; Paul N. Bloom and Brett R. Smith, "Identifying the Drivers of Social Entrepreneurial Impact: Theoretical Development and an Exploratory Empirical Test of SCALERS," *Journal of Social Entrepreneurship* (March 2010), 126–145.

Introduction

1. Michelle Obama, "Remarks at Time 100 Most Influential People Awards" (May 5, 2009) http://www.whitehouse.gov/the_press_office/ Flotus-Remarks-at-Time-100-Most-Influential-People-Awards.
2. http://www.caseatduke.org/knowledge/scalingsocialimpact/.

1 On Your Mark, Get Set, Scale?

1. Paul Brest, "The Power of Theories of Change," *Stanford Social Innovation Review* (Spring 2010), 47–51.
2. "WINGS for Kids," Program of the 2011 Conference on Scaling Social Impact of the Social Impact Exchange (June 15–16, 2011), 46.
3. Source: http://www.changemakers.com/economicopportunity/ entries/4-eyeglasses-poor.
4. "WINGS for Kids," Program of the 2011 Conference on Scaling Social Impact of the Social Impact Exchange (June 15–16, 2011), 46.

5. A. Ahuja, M. Kremer, and A. Peterson-Zwane, "Providing Safe Water: Evidence from Randomized Evaluations," *Annual Review of Resource Economics* (October 2010), 237–256.

6. R. D. Schwartz-Bloom and M. J. Halpin, "Integration of Pharmacology Topics into High School Biology and Chemistry Classes Improves Student Performance," *Journal of Research in Science Teaching* (2003), 922–938.

7. See http://b.3cdn.net/bicycle/43bbbb4ca1493302d6_phm6b0c59.pdf.

8. See http://b.3cdn.net/bicycle/aac4c0fb457fd30689_8em6yo2yv.pdf.

9. See http://www.innonet.org/client_docs/innonet-state-of-evaluation-2010.pdf, and Dean Karlan and Jacob Appel, *More Than Good Intentions* (New York: Penguin Dutton) (2011).

10. See http://www.echoinggreen.org.

11. See http://www.ssireview.org/articles/entry/ten_nonprofit_funding_models.

12. See http://ncat-mbc.org/about/history/.

13. See http://www.pih.org/pages/partners-in-health-history.

14. See http://librariesacrossafrica.org.

15. See http://fenixintl.com.

16. See http://www.coachforcollege.org.

17. See http://www.nytimes.com/2011/06/23/business/smallbusiness/23sbiz.html?pagewanted=all.

18. See http://www.seedschooldc.org.

19. See http://www.trosainc.org.

20. See http://jumpmath1.org.

21. See http://jumpmath1.org/supporting_research.

22. T. Solomon, R. Martinussen, A. Dupuis, S. Gervan, P. Chaban, R. Tannock, B. Ferguson, "Investigation of a Cognitive Science Based Approach to Mathematics Instruction," data presented at the Society for Research in Child Development Biennial Meeting, Montreal (March 31–April 2, 2011).

23. See http://jumpmath1.org/jump_research.

24. See http://www.ashokaglobalizer.org/vision-mission.

25. Source: http://www.yongestreetmedia.ca/innovationnews/jumpmath0427.aspx.

2   Developing a Scaling Strategy That Fits Your Ecosystem

1. "Playworks," Program of the 2011 Conference on Scaling Social Impact of the Social Impact Exchange (June 15–16, 2011), 28–30.

2. "Competing 'Smile' Charities End Disputes and Join Forces," *The Chronicle of Philanthropy* (February 15, 2011).
3. J. Gregory Dees, Beth Battle Anderson, and Jane Wei-Skillern, "Scaling Social Impact," *Stanford Social Innovation Review* (Spring 2004), 24–32 .
4. See http://www.girlsontherun.org and Paul N. Bloom, "Girls on the Run International," Case SE-04, Center for the Advancement of Social Entrepreneurship, Duke University's Fuqua School of Business, (2007), http://www.caseatduke.org/documents/girlsontherun_case.pdf.
5. See http://www.cfy.org/affiliate-network.php.
6. See http://www.cityyear.org/about.aspx.
7. Funda Sezgi and Johanna Mair, "To Control Or Not to Control: A Coordination Perspective to Scaling," in Paul N. Bloom and Edward Skloot, eds., *Scaling Social Impact: New Thinking* (New York: Palgrave Macmillan) (2010), 29–44.
8. See http://www.tostan.org/web/page/592/sectionid/547/pagelevel/3/parentid/585/interior.asp.
9. Michael Rothschild, "Road Crew," in Philip Kotler and Nancy R. Lee, eds., *Social Marketing* (Thousand Oaks, CA: Sage Publications) (2008), 182–185.
10. K. K. Gabriel, R. D. DeBate, R. R. High, and E. F. Racine, "Girls on the Run: A Quasi-Experimental Evaluation of a Developmentally Focused Youth Sport Program," *Journal of Physical Activity & Health* (Volume 8, Supplement, September, 2011), 285–294.
11. See http://www.girlsontherun.org and Paul N. Bloom, "Girls on the Run International," Case SE-04, Center for the Advancement of Social Entrepreneurship, Duke University's Fuqua School of Business, (2007), http://www.caseatduke.org/documents/girlsontherun_case.pdf.

3 Staffing: Building Your Human Resources Capability

1. William H. Draper, *The Startup Game* (New York: Palgrave Macmillan) (2011), 195.
2. See http://www.roomtoread.org.
3. John Wood, quoted in William H. Draper, *The Startup Game* (New York: Palgrave Macmillan) (2011), 202.
4. See http://foundationcenter.org/pnd/ssir/ssir_item.jhtml?id=309700001.
5. W. K. Kellogg Foundation, "Building an Organization to Last: Reflections and Lessons Learned from SeaChange" (July 2003)

http://btw.informingchange.com/uploads/2009/11/Building-an-Organization-to-Last-Reflections-and-Lessons-Learned-from-SeaChange.pdf.

6. "Teach for America," Program of the 2011 Conference on Scaling Social Impact of the Social Impact Exchange (June 15–16, 2011), 31–33.
7. See http://www.challahforhunger.org.
8. See http://prathamindia.blogspot.com.
9. Interview with Jill Vialet, CEO of Playworks, October 19, 2011.
10. See http://www.playworks.org.

4 Communicating: Achieving Buy-In from Key Stakeholders

1. C. H. Denny, J. Tsai, R. L. Floyd, "Alcohol Use Among Pregnant and Nonpregnant Women of Childbearing Age—United States, 1991—2005," *CDC-MMWR* 58 (2009), 529–532.
2. P. A. May, J. P. Gossage, W. O. Kalberg, et al., "Prevalence and Epidemiologic Characteristics of FASD from Various Research Methods with an Emphasis on Recent In-School Studies," *Developmental Disabilities Research Reviews* 15 (2009), 176–192.
3. http://www.hsc.wvu.edu/som/hrc/ECOCWV/PDF/OliverReportFinal.pdf; http://www.jamieoliver.com/us/foundation/jamies-food-revolution/news.
4. Chip Heath and Dan Heath, *Switch* (New York: Broadway Books, 2010).
5. Amy C. Cuddy and K. T. Doherty, "OPOWER: Increasing Energy Efficiency through Normative Influence," Harvard Business School Case N9-911-16.
6. B. L. Anderson, et al., "Knowledge, Opinions, and Practice Patterns of OB-GYNs Regarding their Patients' Use of Alcohol," *Journal of Addiction Medicine* (June 2010), 114–121.
7. F. Foltran, et al., "Effect of Alcohol Consumption in Prenatal Life, Childhood, and Adolescence on Child Development," *Nutrition Reviews* (2011), 642–659, and C. O'Leary and C. Bower, "Guideline for Pregnancy: What's an Acceptable Risk and How is the Evidence (Finally) Shaping Up?" *Drug and Alcohol Review* (2011), online.
8. S. C. Jones and J. Telenta, "What Influences Australian Women to Not Drink Alcohol During Pregnancy," *Australian Journal of Primary Health* (2011), online.

9. http://www.pbs.org/frontlineworld/stories/uganda601.
10. Lauren Trabold, Paul N. Bloom, and Lauren Block, "Communications Strategies for Scaling Health-Focused Social Entrepreneurial Organizations," in Paul N. Bloom and Edward Skloot, eds., *Scaling Social Impact: New Thinking* (New York: Palgrave Macmillan), (2010), 169–188.
11. http://www.m2m.org.
12. Nancy G. Brinker, *Promise Me: How a Sister's Love Launched the Global Movement to End Breast Cancer* (New York: Three Rivers Press) (2010).
13. Maureen O'Donnell, Launching a Brand, http://www.mediabistro.com/portfolios/samples_files/1597991_adBooEn2HXyUBIVgVtOOUqzOL.pdf.
14. Stefano Puntoni, Steven Sweldens, and Nader T. Tavassoli, "Gender Identity Salience and Perceived Vulnerability to Breast Cancer." *Journal of Marketing Research* (2011), 413–424.

5 Alliance-Building: Creating Synergies with Others

1. Lisa E. Bolton, Paul N. Bloom, and Joel B. Cohen, "Using Loan Plus Lender Literacy Information to Combat One-Sided Marketing of Debt Consolidation Loans," *Journal of Marketing Research* (2011), S51-S59.
2. http://www.caseatduke.org/documents/Childfinance_Duke_Case_Study.pdf.
3. Jon Huggett, *Jazz, Not Symphony* (New York: Palgrave-Macmillan) (in press).
4. James E. Austin, *The Collaboration Challenge* (San Francisco: Jossey-Bass, 2000).
5. Shirley Sagawa and Eli Segal, *Common Interest, Common Good* (Boston: Harvard Business School Press, 2000).
6. Shuili Du, Sankar Sen, and C. B. Bhattacharya, "Exploring the Social and Business Returns of a Corporate Oral Health Initiative Aimed at Disadvantaged Hispanic Families," *Journal of Consumer Research* (2008), 483–494.
7. http://www.accionusa.org/home/small-business-loans/about-our-loans/brewing-the-american-dream-loan-fund.aspx.
8. Paul N. Bloom, Steve Hoeffler, Kevin Lane Keller, and Carlos E. Basurto Meza, "How Social-Cause Marketing Affects Consumer

Perceptions," *MIT Sloan Management Review* (Winter 2006), 49–55.

9. http://www.worldtoilet.org.
10. The material in this section is drawn from the KaBOOM website (http://www.kaboom.org) and from the autobiography written by KaBOOM's founder: Darell Hammond, *KaBOOM: How One Man Built a Movement to Save Play* (Emmaus, PA: Rodale Press, 2011).

6   Lobbying: Using Advocacy to Create Social Change Opportunities

1. See http://www.youthbuild.org.
2. See http://www.benetech.org/download/landmines-lessons_2007.pdf.
3. See http://www.madd.org/laws.
4. See http://www.fairtradetownsusa.org/towns.
5. The material in this section is drawn from the Campaign for Tobacco-Free Kids website (http://www.tobaccofreekids.org) and from the book written by the Campaign's founder: Bill Novelli, *50+: Igniting a Revolution to Reinvent America* (New York: St. Martin's Press, 2006).
6. Bill Novelli, *50+: Igniting a Revolution to Reinvent America* (New York: St. Martin's Press, 2006), 183.

7   Earnings-Generation: Attracting and Replenishing Financial Resources

1. See www.driptech.com.
2. See http://www.livemint.com/2010/12/16220907/MFIs-hit-as-repayment-rate-slu.html?atype=tp.
3. See http://www.redf.org.
4. See http://www.trosainc.org.
5. See http://www.specialistpeople.com.
6. See http://www.riders.org/us/n_details.aspx?nwId=251.
7. See http://www.newmansown.com/camps.aspx.
8. Address by Linda Lee at the "Marketing, Corporate Social Initiatives, and the Bottom Line" Workshop held at the University of North Carolina at Chapel Hill on March 14, 2001, sponsored by the Marketing Science Institute.
9. See http://www.hopeconsulting.us.
10. See http://www.redf.org.

11. See http://www.ourgreenstreets.org.
12. See http://www.buckelew.org.
13. See http://www.solutionssf.org.
14. See http://peoplesharvest.org.
15. See http://www.redf.org/donate/messengerbag.
16. See http://numitea.com/people/communitea/#philanthropy/
17. Personal correspondence from Carla Javits, President of REDF.
18. Personal correspondence from Carla Javits, President of REDF.

8 Replicating: Creating Evidence and Systems to Support More of the Same

1. See http://www.citizenschools.org/news/press-release-external-study-finds-citizen-schools-students-significantly-outperform-peers.
2. See http://www.cesolutions.org.
3. See http://www.kickstart.org/what-we-do/process/step-04.php.
4. See http://www.aflatoun.org/?mission-history.
5. See http://www.aflatoun.org/?factsfigures.
6. See http://aflatoun.org/downloads/aflatoun-strategic-plan-2008–2010.pdf.
7. See http://aflatoun.org/downloads/children-and-change-2010.pdf.
8. See http://www.aflatoun.org/?curriculum.

9 Stimulating Market Forces: Getting Incentives to Work for You

1. See http://www.msc.org.
2. See http://www.bcorporation.net.
3. See Kathi Jaworski, "Social Impact Bonds No Cure All for Nonprofits," *Nonprofit Newswire* (June 21, 2011). See http://www.nonprofitquarterly.org/index.php?option=com_content&view=article&id=13361:social-impact-bonds-no-cure-all-for-nonprofits&catid=155:nonprofit-newswire&Itemid=986.
4. David Bornstein, "Instead of Student Loans, Investing in Futures," http://opinionator.blogs.nytimes.com/2011/05/30/instead-of-student-loans-investing-in-futures/.
5. See http://www.fire-hose.co.uk.
6. The material in this section is drawn from the Fair Trade USA website (http://www.fairtradeusa.org) and interviews with members of their staff.

10 Putting It All Together: Embracing Contingencies and Complexity

1. See Paul N. Bloom and Brett R. Smith, "Identifying the Drivers of Social Entrepreneurial Impact: Theoretical Development and an Exploratory Empirical Test of SCALERS," *Journal of Social Entrepreneurship* (March 2010), 126–145; Paul N. Bloom et al., "Scaling Social Impact: A Replication and Extension of SCALERS," presentation at the Research Colloquium in Social Entrepreneurship, Duke University (June 2011); Sophie Bacq et al., "Governing for Efficiency within Social Entrepreneurial Ventures: The Mediating Role of Organizational Capabilities," presentation at the Research Colloquium in Social Entrepreneurship, Duke University (June 2011).

Index